Rhoda Red and Loretta Legg

Working with Fives and Tens

Catherine Twomey Fosnot
Janan Hamm

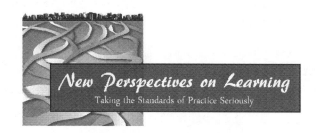

New Perspectives on Learning, LLC
1194 Ocean Avenue
New London, CT 06320

ISBN-13: 978-1-7320437-0-1

Table of Contents

Unit Overview 2

Day 1 – Are They All Here?...11
Students read *are You All Here?* and learn about Rhoda Red, modeling the possible arrangements of her 5 chicks on a 5-bead Mathrack™.

Day 2 – Equivalence...19
After a minilesson using quick images, students complete and then share their work arranging the chicks in a gallery walk and math congress.

Day 3 – Finding Five Chicks 24
A minilesson provides an opportunity to discuss strategies for finding the number of chicks and students play a game: *Finding Five Chicks.*

Day 4 – Fish for Fives 29
After a quick minilesson, students play a new game matching expressions that make 5: *Fish for Fives*.

Day 5 – How Many Are Hiding?..34
A minilesson challenges children to find the missing addends and then students play *Building Equations.*

Day 6 – Is the Gang of Ten All Here? 38
Students read *The Gang's All Here* and explore ways to arrange 10 chicks, 5 red and 5 white.

Day 7 – Equivalence Revisited...41
After a minilesson using the 10-bead Mathrack™, students complete and then share their work arranging the chicks in a gallery walk and math congress.

Day 8 – Rolling for Fives and Tens 45
After another minilesson using the 10-bead Mathrack™, students arrange dice to build expressions totaling 5 or 10 in the game *Rolling for Fives and Tens.*

Day 9 – Barnyard Match 49
Students find the missing addends in a minilesson and then make matches adding to 10 in *Barnyard Match.*

Day 10 – Fish for Tens 53
A minilesson encourages students to imagine how missing addends would look on an arithmetic rack and then they play a final match-making game: *Fish for Tens.*

Appendices..58

Unit Overview

This unit begins with the story of Rhoda Red—a Rhode Island Red mother hen—and her five chicks. As the chicks play in the barnyard, a crafty old fox eyes them and decides a chick might be a fine dinner. The mother hen becomes increasingly nervous trying to watch her chicks. First, she sees all 5 in a line, but then 3 and 2, 4 and 1, and 2 and 3! Are they still all there?

The context of Rhoda's chicks is used to support the development of several big ideas related to early number sense: cardinality, equivalence, compensation, conservation, commutativity, and associativity. The context is also used to introduce the 5-bead arithmetic rack: a powerful model that supports the development of part-whole relations as children develop early number sense. A significant body of research now provides evidence that small amounts— 1, 2, and 3—can be subitized at birth, or at least as close to birth as we can reliably test (Dehaene, 1999). These amounts do not need to be counted; they can be seen at a glance as similar or different. Babies can even tell when one object is missing! As young PK-K children grapple to explain that 3+2 is equal to 2+3, and that 4+1 can also be 2+2+1, they eventually come to understand that 5 is an amount, not the name of the object touched last when counting to 5. Eventually they stop counting the beads on the Mathrack™, just trusting that 5 are there, and they become able to see 5 inside of 6 or 7. They "prioritize" the five.

Once the 5-structure is prioritized and the 5 beads are understood as an amount, counting becomes unnecessary and the 10-bead rack (comprised of 5 red and 5 white beads) can be used. In the second week of the unit, the read-aloud *The Gang's All Here* is used to introduce the 10-bead rack. Loretta Leghorn, a large white hen and a friend of Rhoda Red's, gives birth to 5 white chicks. Now the two mother hens have 10 chicks to keep track of—not an easy task for the two mother hens (or your young kindergarteners)! The 10-bead Mathrack™ (and the context of the 10 chicks) is used to support the development of mental imagery of 6 as 5+1, 7 as 5+2, etc. Images like these with the 5 inside the total amount support the understanding that if 5+5 = 10, then 6+4 and 7+3 must also be 10 because of compensation and associativity—a bead has just moved over. Also, now the white beads can be subitized: if 2 white beads are shown with the 5 red (as an image of 7), then only 3 white beads remain on the right.

This unit only makes use of these first two racks: the five and the ten. You will want to do concentrated work with the 5- and 10-racks until children no longer count before introducing the 20-bead rack. Ensure that your children "just know" 7 is 5+2, and that they trust that the group of 5 is inside and does not need to be counted. Once the 5- and 10-structures are prioritized you can move on to using the 20-bead rack. That rack is introduced later with the unit *Bunk Beds and Apple Boxes.*

Rhoda Red and Loretta Leghorn is designed to align with the CCSS Standards of Mathematical Practice and the following core objectives:

Counting & Cardinality.K.CC: Count to tell the number of objects.

CCSS.MATH.CONTENT.K.CC.B.4.B

Understand that the last number name said tells the number of objects counted. The number of objects is the same regardless of their arrangement or the order in which they were counted.

CCSS.MATH.CONTENT.K.CC.B.4.C

Understand that each successive number name refers to a quantity that is one larger.

Counting & Cardinality.K.CC: Compare numbers.

CCSS.MATH.CONTENT.K.CC.C.6

Identify whether the number of objects in one group is greater than, less than, or equal to the number of objects in another group, e.g., by using matching and counting strategies.[1]

CCSS.MATH.CONTENT.K.CC.C.7

Compare two numbers between 1 and 10 presented as written numerals.

Operations & Algebraic Thinking.K.OA: Understand addition as putting together and adding to, and understand subtraction as taking apart and taking from.

CCSS.MATH.CONTENT.K.OA.A.1

Represent addition and subtraction with objects, fingers, mental images, drawings[1], sounds (e.g., claps), acting out situations, verbal explanations, expressions, or equations.

CCSS.MATH.CONTENT.K.OA.A.2

Solve addition and subtraction word problems, and add and subtract within 10, e.g., by using objects or drawings to represent the problem.

CCSS.MATH.CONTENT.K.OA.A.3

Decompose numbers less than or equal to 10 into pairs in more than one way, e.g., by using objects or drawings, and record each decomposition by a drawing or equation (e.g., 5 = 2+3 and 5 = 4+1).

CCSS.MATH.CONTENT.K.OA.A.4

For any number from 1 to 9, find the number that makes 10 when added to the given number, e.g., by using objects or drawings, and record the answer with a drawing or equation.

CCSS.MATH.CONTENT.K.OA.A.5

Fluently add and subtract within 5.

The Landscape of Learning

BIG IDEAS
❖ Cardinality
❖ One-to-one correspondence
❖ Hierarchical inclusion
❖ Compensation and equivalence
❖ Conservation
❖ Commutativity
❖ Associativity
STRATEGIES
❖ Subitizes 1, 2, and 3
❖ Synchrony and one-to-one tagging
❖ Counting three times
❖ Counting on
❖ Prioritizing the five
❖ Using compensation and associativity
❖ Using commutativity
❖ Systematic production of arrangements
MODELS
❖ 5-bead arithmetic rack
❖ 10-bead arithmetic rack
❖ 5-structure
❖ 10-structure

The Mathematical Landscape

The mathematical focus of *Rhoda Red and Loretta Leghorn: Working with Fives and Tens* is early number sense. This unit is the first in a series designed to generate the arithmetic rack model. Developed by Adri Treffers, a researcher at the Freudenthal Institute in The Netherlands, the rack supports children to prioritize the 5 and 10 structures, enabling them to move away from counting one by one to decomposing and composing number with sub-units (Treffers, 1991). Once children can image 7 as composed of 5+2, and 5 as 2+3, they become able to see 7+3 as 10. Later in development they become able to see 7+7 as (5+2)+(5+2) = 10+4.

As young children explore the investigations within this unit, several big ideas will likely arise. These include:

- ❖ *Cardinality*
- ❖ *One-to-one correspondence*
- ❖ *Hierarchical inclusion*
- ❖ *Compensation and equivalence*
- ❖ *Conservation*
- ❖ *Commutativity*
- ❖ *Associativity*

❖ *Cardinality*

Young children often count by rote without understanding the purpose of counting. They may not have constructed the big idea of **cardinality**—that the number they end on is the amount of the set of objects. Thus, it is important when children finish counting to ask, "So how many do you have?" Don't assume that because they seem to count well that they understand that 5 means five objects. They may think the fifth bead is 5.

❖ *One-to-one correspondence*

Children also may not have constructed the big idea of **one-to-one correspondence**—that if there is a corresponding object matched to each one in the set, the totals are equivalent. For example, if there are 5 chicks, 5 beads will correspond in a one-to-one fashion.

❖ *Hierarchical inclusion*

Even when children do understand cardinality and one-to-one correspondence, they may still not realize that the numbers grow by one, and exactly one, each time. Researchers call this idea **hierarchical inclusion**. They mean that amounts nest inside each other: 6 includes 5, plus 1 more; 5 includes 4, plus 1 more, etc.

❖ *Compensation and equivalence*

Children may also have a difficult time comprehending that 5+5 is equivalent to 4+6. The big ideas here are **compensation and equivalence**—that if you lose one (from the first 5, for example) but gain it (onto the other 5), the total stays the same. The amounts may look different, but they are equivalent.

❖ Conservation

It is the construction of the justifications of compensation and reversibility (what has been moved can be moved back) that bring children to conclude amounts have been conserved. If nothing has been added or removed (only moved around) the amount is the same—counting again is unnecessary.

❖ Commutativity

If the order of two addends is reversed, the total amount is conserved. Young children often call this the "turn around rule" or the "switch-a-roo." "If you turn numbers around," they say, "the answer is still the same." The commutative property holds for addition.

❖ Associativity

The associative property of addition is just the generalization of compensation: if you give whatever you remove from one addend to the other, then the total amount is conserved. The associative property holds for addition: numbers can be decomposed and associated in a variety of ways and the sum is still the same.

STRATEGIES

As you work with the activities in this unit, you will notice that students will use many strategies to solve the problems that are posed to them. Here are some strategies to notice:

- ❖ **Subitizes 1, 2, and 3**
- ❖ **Synchrony and one-to-one tagging**
- ❖ **Counting three times**
- ❖ **Counting on**
- ❖ **Prioritizing the 5**
- ❖ **Using compensation and associativity**
- ❖ **Using commutativity**
- ❖ **Systematic production of arrangements**

❖ Subitizes 1, 2, and 3

The ability to see 1, 2, and 3 as sub-units is purely perceptual. Children most likely have this ability at birth. However, even though you won't have to develop it, we have listed it so that you notice it and encourage children to use what they know. Too often, well-meaning teachers tell children to count to figure out a total, and children thus unfortunately abandon the use of subitizing.

❖ Synchrony and one-to-one tagging

Counting effectively requires children to coordinate many actions simultaneously. Not only must they remember the word that comes next, they must use only one word for each object (**synchrony**) and tag each object once and only once (**one-to-one tagging**). When children are initially learning to count this coordination is very difficult; they often skip some objects, double-tag others, and their actions are not synchronized. They use too many or too few words for the number of objects they are counting.

❖ Counting three times

Making groups and determining the total amount is a huge undertaking. To determine the total of an arrangement, children may tediously **count three times**—first each of the two groups and then the whole, starting from 1 each time. For example, to see if 3 chicks and 2 chicks are still 5 chicks, they may count 1 through 3, 1 through 2, and then 1 through 5.

❖ Counting on

A major landmark strategy to notice and celebrate is when a child begins to **count on**—labeling the first set "5," and then continuing: "...6, 7."

❖ Prioritizing the 5

As children come to trust and prioritize the 5 as a group on the 10-rack, you will find that they no longer count it. They just say "5," and then count on. This should be celebrated! It is a developmental advance, as big as the movement from crawling to walking!

❖ Using compensation and associativity

As children construct the big ideas of compensation and associativity, they begin to use them to efficiently make equivalent arrangements. They will turn 7+3 into 6+4 and won't even need to count.

❖ Using commutativity

Children will also use commutativity. If they have found that 3+2 = 5, to find another arrangement that also equals 5 they just switch the numbers, yielding 2+3 = 5.

❖ Systematic production of arrangements

Often children begin to make equivalent arrangements by using **trial and error**. However, once children construct the big ideas of compensation and equivalence, that 5+5 = 4+6, and hierarchical inclusion, that numbers nest inside each other and grow by 1 each time, a major change in strategy may occur as they use these ideas to **generate all the possibilities systematically**—turning 9+1 into 8+2, then 7+3, etc.

Initially models emerge as a representation *of* a situation; later they are used by teachers to represent children's computation strategies. Ultimately, they are appropriated by children as powerful tools *for* thinking (Gravemeijer, 1999). Models go through three stages of development (Gravemeijer, 1999; Fosnot and Dolk, 2001): modeling of the situation, modeling by the teacher of the children's strategies, and models as tools for thinking.

❖ *Model of the situation*

The models introduced in this unit are the 5-bead and 10-bead arithmetic racks. With the rack children are supported to envision the part-whole relations of number with five and ten as special units. The rack's features—two colors and the ability to slide the beads—allow children to initially **model the situation** by moving beads to the right and to the left to represent the movement of the chicks in the barnyard.

❖ *Model of children's strategies*

Once the model has been introduced to represent the situation, you can use it to **model the children's strategies** as they determine arrangements. If a child counts by ones, move one bead at a time; if a child counts on, move the set, then move beads one at a time onto the set. If a child uses compensation, remove a bead from one group and slide it onto the other group.

❖ *Model as a tool for thinking*

Eventually children will be able to use this model **as a tool for thinking** (Gravemeijer, 1999)—they will be able to imagine 6+4 being turned into 5+5. Although beyond the purpose of this unit, over time the arithmetic rack will become an important model to support children to develop automaticity of the basic facts for addition and subtraction (Treffers, 1991).

Many opportunities will arise to discuss these landmarks as you work through the unit. Look for moments of puzzlement. Don't be afraid to let children discuss their ideas and check and recheck their counting. Celebrate their accomplishments just like you would the development of their first steps when they learned to walk.

A graphic of the full landscape of learning for early number sense, addition and subtraction follows. The purpose of the graphic is to enable you to see the longer journey of development and to place your work with this unit within the scope of this long-term development. You may also find it helpful to use this graphic to record for yourself the progress of individual children. Each landmark can be shaded in as you find evidence in a child's work and in the things said—evidence that a child has constructed the landmark strategies and big ideas. [Note: An assessment app with a digital version of the landscape is also available from www.NewPerspectivesOnAssessment.com.] In a sense you will be recording the individual pathways children take as they develop as young mathematicians.

References and Resources

Dehaene, Stanislaus. 1999. *The Number Sense: How the Mind Creates Mathematics.* New York, NY: Oxford University Press.

Fosnot, Catherine Twomey, and Maarten Dolk. 2001. *Young Mathematicians at Work: Constructing Early Number Sense, Addition and Subtraction.* Portsmouth, NH: Heinemann.

Gravemeijer, Koeno P. E. 1999. How emergent models may foster the constitution of formal mathematics. *Mathematical Thinking and Learning 1* (2): 155–77.

Treffers, Adri. 1991. Rekenen tot twentig met het rekenrek [Calculating to twenty with the arithmetic rack]. *Willem Bartjens* 10 (1): 35-45.

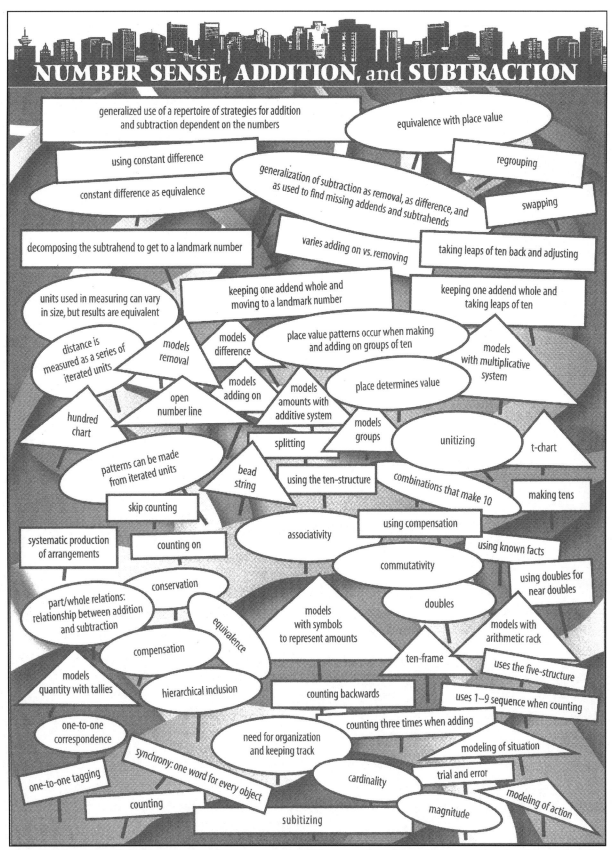

NUMBER SENSE, ADDITION, and SUBTRACTION

generalized use of a repertoire of strategies for addition and subtraction dependent on the numbers

equivalence with place value

using constant difference

regrouping

constant difference as equivalence

generalization of subtraction as removal, as difference, and as used to find missing addends and subtrahends

swapping

decomposing the subtrahend to get to a landmark number

varies adding on vs. removing

taking leaps of ten back and adjusting

units used in measuring can vary in size, but results are equivalent

keeping one addend whole and moving to a landmark number

keeping one addend whole and taking leaps of ten

distance is measured as a series of iterated units

models removal

models difference

place value patterns occur when making and adding on groups of ten

models with multiplicative system

models adding on

models amounts with additive system

place determines value

open number line

hundred chart

models groups

unitizing

t-chart

patterns can be made from iterated units

splitting

bead string

using the ten-structure

combinations that make 10

making tens

skip counting

systematic production of arrangements

counting on

associativity

using compensation

using known facts

conservation

commutativity

using doubles for near doubles

part/whole relations: relationship between addition and subtraction

equivalence

compensation

models with symbols to represent amounts

doubles

models with arithmetic rack

ten-frame

uses the five-structure

models quantity with tallies

hierarchical inclusion

counting backwards

uses 1–9 sequence when counting

one-to-one correspondence

counting three times when adding

need for organization and keeping track

modeling of situation

one-to-one tagging

synchrony: one word for every object

cardinality

trial and error

modeling of action

counting

magnitude

subitizing

The landscape of learning: number sense, addition, and subtraction on the horizon showing landmark strategies (rectangles), big ideas (ovals), and models (triangles).

DAY ONE

ARE THEY ALL HERE?

Materials Needed

Are You All Here?
[A full-color version is available from Amazon, but if you do not have it you can use Appendix A.]

Class-size 5-bead Mathrack™ (available from www.Mathrack.com)

Individual 5-bead Mathracks™ (one per pair of students, available from www.Mathrack.com)

Drawing paper and markers or pencils

Glue sticks, one per pair of students

Scissors, one per pair of students

Rhoda's Chicks (Appendix B, one set per student)

The story *Are You All Here?* sets the stage for investigating various arrangements of five chicks playing in the barnyard as their anxious mother tries to make sure none of the chicks have been eaten by the fox. After the children hear the story and act it out on the 5-bead Mathrack™, they go off to investigate finding, and recording, various possible arrangements of the 5 chicks. The 5-bead Mathrack™ and the baby chick context are used to support the development of equivalence and compensation. For example, the situation of 3 chicks on the left and 2 chicks on the right side of the barnyard is explored as being equivalent to 4 chicks on the left and 1 chick on the right; 1 chick has just moved.

Day One Outline

Developing the Context
❖ Read the story *Are You All Here?*
❖ Introduce the 5-bead Mathrack™ and help children to act out the story using it.

Supporting the Investigation
❖ Note children's strategies as they explore different ways the chicks might be arranged in the barnyard. Confer by celebrating their attempts and challenging them to find other equivalent arrangements.

Developing the Context

Read *Are You All Here?* (Appendix A). Allow children to discuss their ideas about whether all the chicks are in the barnyard as you are reading the story. The purpose of the reading is to draw children's attention to the idea that five chicks can be arranged in ways that look very different but that are still the same five chicks.

Introduce the 5-bead Mathrack™, using it to model the situations in the read-aloud. Note the similarity of the five red chicks to the five red beads on the rack and ask the children how they think it might look if you used the rack to retell and act out some of Rhoda's puzzling moments in the story. Make sure students agree that 5 red beads can be used to represent 5 red chicks. This assumption requires 1-1 correspondence and for those who have yet to construct this idea it may not be apparent.

As you retell the story, ask children to share how they know the chicks are still all there in each scenario. Use the 5-rack to model children's strategies as they share. For example, if a child counts, move one bead at a time as he counts. If a child counts on, slide the group she starts with over with one push, treating it as a group, and then count on. If a child says that 3+2 is the same as 2+3, turn the rack over to show how order does not matter (commutativity). If a child says, 3+2 is equal to 4+1 because one of the chicks just moved, show 3 beads on the left and 2 beads on the right and then slowly move 1 bead from the right to the left to produce 4+1 (compensation and associativity).

> **Teacher Note**
>
> Some teachers choose to read the entire story during a read-aloud time and then during math workshop they revisit the story and have students retell and act out important moments with the Mathrack™ to launch the investigation. Others use the story at the start of the investigation, and stop for discussion at the moments in the story where the text invites conversation: *are they all here?* The modeling with the Mathrack™ is then incorporated as the story is being read. Either approach is fine.

After a discussion about a few of the students' favorite moments where the chicks were playing tricks on their mother, share with children that they have made you curious about whether there might be any other tricks those chicks could play. Suggest they work with a partner to investigate and see if they can figure out ways the chicks could fool their mother by being in different groups, but still being 5 altogether. Invite them to tell their own stories of different ways the 5 chicks can arrange themselves. Pass out copies of Appendix B, glue sticks, pencils (or markers), individual 5-racks, scissors, and paper. Have the students cut out groups of chicks from Appendix B and glue them onto a separate sheet of paper. Support them to write equations on their drawings and to model the action on an individual 5-bead Mathrack™ with their math partner.

[Note: You can give students larger drawing paper or several sheets of 8.5 x 11 paper to illustrate their ideas. If you use drawing paper, they will likely be able to do several arrangements on one piece. If you use 8.5 x 11 copy paper, have them do one arrangement on each piece. These can then be stapled together into a book for each child to take home.]

Inside One Classroom: Developing the Context

Anna (the teacher): I brought a tool to help us think about the story of Rhoda Red and her chicks. What do you see? Does this tool remind you of our story?

Ming: The beads are red just like the chicks.

Liam: (*Excitedly, as Anna casually moves a group of 2 beads from the left side of the 5-bead rack to the right*) The beads move around just like the chicks!

Anna: Yun, can you show the class the thinking you were showing me with your fingers? (*Yun raises two hands, one showing 3 fingers and the other 2 fingers.*) Who thinks they know what Yun is trying to show?

Hameed: That's just 3 and 2.

Anna: Yun, is that what you were thinking? You just know 3, (*pointing to the hand with 3 fingers*) and 2 (*pointing to the hand with 2 fingers*)? (*Yun nods affirmatively.*) Who else thinks they might know what Yun is thinking?

Emma: (*Pointing at the picture of the chicks on the cover of the book*) Yun is showing the babies. (*Yun enthusiastically nods yes.*)

Anna: So, if we have moved 3 beads over here (*moving the 3 from right to left, and then back again left to right*), how many are left over here (*pointing to the 2 on the children's left*)?

(*Yun holds up 2 fingers.*)

Anna: 2, right Yun! So just like you said, Emma and Hameed... It is 3 and 2. How many chicks is that? Are they all here, or did the fox get one? Everyone, turn and talk to your elbow partner about this. If there are 3 here and 2 over there, are all 5 here, or did the fox get one? (*Anna moves around and listens in to several conversations as partners talk and then she resumes whole group conversation.*) Put your thumb up if you think all 5 are there. Put your thumb down if you think some might be missing. And wave your thumb if you are not sure.

Author's notes

Notice how Anna is supporting the conversation between the students by asking them to consider what each might be thinking.

Some young children may need to physically move their bodies or use their fingers to act out the story to help them think about and discuss how the situation might look on the 5-bead rack. Many children will be able to use their innate perceptual ability to subitize (see small amounts as wholes) to describe the groups of chicks, but others may not be able to talk about what they see and will respond by counting each group. Anna supports Yun, a recent arrival from China, with the social knowledge of the words.

(Anna notes that some children are counting; others know 3+2 are 5, and still others are waving thumbs showing that they don't know.) Emma, I see you counting. Can you count out loud for us?

Emma: 1, 2, 3... (Anna helps with the social knowledge of the language, offering "4...") 4, 5.

Anna: So how many chicks is that?

(Emma starts to count again.) Wait, before you count again... does anyone know? Emma said 1, 2, 3, 4, 5. How many chicks is that? Hameed?

Hameed: 5. 3 over there and 2 over here. Like Yun showed with his fingers.

Anna: Do you think there are 5, Yun? (Yun nods and puts 3 fingers up and then 2.) So, what if I move 1 bead over to this side of the rack? Now it is 2 over on this side and 3 over here. Is it still 5 chicks?

Hameed: Still 5. One chick just moved over there to play. The fox didn't get any.

Anna: So, it sounds like you think there are lots of different ways for the chicks to move around and play, and even though it looks different it is still 5? (Several children nod affirmatively, but others are not sure.) So, let's explore this some. I'm going to give everyone a rack and some drawing paper. Work with your math partner and make some pictures of how the 5 chicks might move. I wonder if there are a lot of ways, or just a few? Let's think of all the ways we can.

Several big ideas are at play here: cardinality and conservation. Note how Anna lets Emma count but then she asks how many that is. When Emma starts to count again, Anna stops her and asks if anyone knows without needing to count again. Moves like this bring cardinality to the fore for consideration. "Five" is not just a counting word—it is an amount.

Anna turns back to Yun and supports him further. Then she challenges students by moving one over. Now the big idea of compensation is also under discussion.

The storyline is now clear to the children and they are ready to go off and draw stories about the 5 chicks moving. The Mathracks™ are available to model the situations they imagine; they are tools for thinking.

Supporting the Investigation

As students begin to work, make a quick scan of the room to make sure all students are engaged. If some students are not engaged, check first to make sure they understand the context. With partners who are not clear about what to do, you might suggest that they take turns visualizing an arrangement of the chicks that Rhoda Red might see in the barnyard and show it to their partner on the 5-bead Mathrack™. Suggest that it can be hard to remember all the arrangements they might come up with, so they will need to show each of the arrangements they make on their drawing paper. Provide multiple copies of the strips of the 5 chicks and explain that you have extra copies as well if they need more. Once a partnership agrees on an arrangement that might fool Rhoda, they should cut out the chicks from the strip to match their groupings and arrange and paste them on the drawing paper. For children who are ready to write numerals, you can encourage them to write their story in a math statement: for example, if they have started with 3+2 and had a chick leave the 3 and go over to the 2 chicks on the other side, thereby making 2+3, you might encourage them to write "3+2 = 2+3." If children have only shown an arrangement and not shown the movement, you might concentrate on the cardinality of the arrangement and help them write, "3+2 = 5."

Once most students are fully engaged, take note of the strategies you see and choose a few pairs to sit and confer with. You will likely see several strategies like those shown in Figures 1-3. Figure 1 shows an example of work that at first glance may suggest cardinality has not yet been constructed. But, note how the equations are written differently. At the bottom there is no plus sign between the last two 1s. A dialogue box follows as a teacher confers with this pair. In it you can study how powerful a conferral can be when teachers hold off on making judgments and work first to clarify for themselves what learners are doing. Once clarification is achieved, the conferral is characterized by cycles of celebrating and challenging.

Figure 1. The Work Being Discussed in the Dialogue Box.

Anna (the teacher): I noticed that this one on the bottom seems to be the same as the first arrangement you made. But, I also noticed that you put the plus sign at the end. Is there a reason you did that?

Jade: Yes. Two chicks are together. We are going to cut out a group of two, right Maya?

Anna: Oh! That is interesting. So, you decided you could put two of your ones together to make a new arrangement? Now you have 1+1+1+2? That's a terrific idea! You are combining and recombining your ones? What will you do next?

Maya: We are going to make the 3 ones into a group of 3. Then we will have 3+2.

Anna: Wow! This idea of grouping the chicks using your ones is a super idea! But what will you do next to make another way? *(Both girls now look puzzled.)* I wonder if you could move some of the chicks? Did you explore this on the mathrack? *(Anna picks up the 5-bead rack and places 3 beads on the left and 2 on the right.)* This is what you are thinking of making, right?

Jade: Maybe we could move one chick from there to the other group? *(She moves 1 from the group of 3 to the group of 2, effectively turning 3+2 into 2 +3. Maya starts to count by ones to check.)*

Anna: Wait, before you count let's think about this. You had 3 chicks here and 2 there and Jade just made one chick go to the other group, right? Are the chicks still all there? Did you take any chicks away, Jade?

Jade: No. They are all there. I just moved one over there *(pointing to the original group of 2, which is now 3).*

Maya: Oh, I get it! That's what the chicks were doing in the story to fool the mom!

Anna: Wow. This is a great strategy! You have your ones and you are just moving them around. I wonder if you can find all the ways the chicks can group themselves with this strategy? How will you know if you get duplicates? Can you find a way to keep track?

Author's notes

Note how Anna does not focus on getting the plus sign moved, nor does she assume the children's representation of 3 chicks with the numeral 5 is wrong. She begins the conferral by clarifying for herself what the children are doing. Rather than "red-penning" or fixing the piece of work, she focuses on the development of her young mathematicians. Now that she understands they are combining and recombining ones, she celebrates their idea and then challenges them to find other groupings.

The Mathrack™ is a helpful tool for thinking.

Anna celebrates and challenges further: How can one keep track? Can this strategy be used to find all the possible ways?

Figure 2. The Commutative Property.

The work in Figure 2 shows evidence of the commutative property. The children have written 4+1 and then 1+4. However, without conferring there is no way to know if that idea was consciously used, if it is a generalizable idea for them, or whether they will continue using it as they proceed. Asking these children if it is okay to reverse the order when adding, or whether doing so might change the answer, is an important conferral move. If the students can defend the switching of the addends, ask them if it would be a helpful strategy to continue with. Once commutativity is justified (usually just by turning the rack), you might ask, "Is it ok for the 1 to just move over, too? Questioning along these lines might help them notice associativity as well–that the 1 can be moved over: $(2+1) + 2 = 2 + (1+2)$.

Figure 3. Compensation and the Associative Property.

The work shown in Figure 3 is also a sample of the type of work you will want to confer on. It is possible that the students have just worked randomly and found several arrangements that work. But, it is also possible that they began by working systematically using compensation and then abandoned the idea. Young children often get distracted and forget the idea they started with. Either way, these students would likely benefit from an encouragement to model their arrangements on the 5-bead rack. You might ask, "How did 3+2 become 4+1?" And then, "How did that arrangement become 5+0?" This may not be the order in which the arrangements were made, but a conferral on how the arrangements are related might support the development of compensation and associativity.

Reflections on the Day

Today, children were introduced to several big ideas about number. Within the context of baby chicks moving around in the barnyard, they explored conservation, compensation, equivalence, and cardinality. They were also introduced to the 5-bead Mathrack™, which over time will become a powerful tool to help them prioritize the 5-structure. On Day Two they will have opportunities to continue their work and a congress will be held providing for a discussion on some of the big ideas that emerged.

DAY TWO

EQUIVALENCE

Materials Needed

Are You All Here? [If you do not have the full-color version, you can use Appendix A.]

Quick Images Cards (Appendix C)

Class-size 5-bead Mathrack™

Individual 5-bead racks (one per pair of students)

Students' work from Day One

Several sheets of copy or drawing paper and markers or pencils

Glue sticks, one per pair of students

Scissors, one per pair of students

Rhoda's Chicks (Appendix B, several extra sets)

Today begins with a minilesson as a warm-up to math workshop. Students work with a string of related images designed to support the development of the commutative property. After the minilesson, students are given an opportunity to revisit their thinking from Day One, and to revise or add on to their work in preparation for a gallery walk and congress. The focus of the congress is equivalence.

Day Two Outline

Minilesson: A String of Related Problems
❖ Use the set of quick images provided in Appendix C. Show one at a time and invite discussion of strategies.
❖ Use the class-size 5-bead Mathrack™ to represent student strategies.

Supporting the Investigation:
❖ Remind students of the story *Are You All Here?* and provide students with time to revisit their work from yesterday and to revise as they wish in preparation for a gallery walk and congress.

Facilitating the Gallery Walk
❖ Post student work around the room and invite review.

Facilitating the Math Congress
❖ Invite two or three pairs to share their work to the group
❖ Foster discussion on some big ideas related to equivalence that emerged from the landscape, for example commutativity or compensation and associativity. Use the class-size 5-bead Mathrack™ to model strategies and big ideas during the discussion.

Minilesson: A String of Related Problems

Use the set of quick image cards provided on Appendix C. Show one image at a time in the order below and invite students to determine how many chicks are on the cards. As strategies are shared for determining the total number of chicks, use the class-size 5-bead Mathrack™ to represent student thinking. To represent commutativity, the rack can just be turned (or flipped) 180 degrees as shown below.

The String:
5 on the left
   3+2
   2+3
   1+4
   4+1
5 on the right

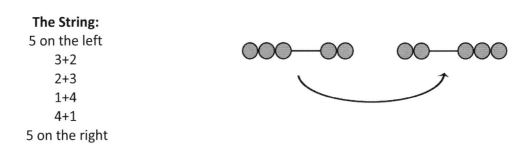

Teacher Note

The string is designed to support the development of commutativity. Let children feel like they have invented this big idea. Don't explain it ahead; just adopt the terminology of the children who first offer the idea. At this young age the formal name *commutative property* is not necessary. Children often name it "the turnaround" or they say, "order doesn't matter."

Many teachers name strategies after the child who first offers it and justifies it, explaining that mathematicians love naming things after themselves. A practice like this builds empowerment and competence. You can build a strategy wall to display all the "inventions" children have discovered and justified throughout the year. Having a wall of strategies on display allows children to revisit, reflect on, and use previously justified ideas and strategies. And, they feel very proud to have their inventions on display.

Supporting the Investigation

Remind students of the story *Are You All Here?* Explain that the class will have a gallery walk to look at each other's work but that you want to provide time first in case anyone wants to add on to what they did yesterday, revise, or write more about strategies they discovered. Suggest that the minilesson might even have provided ideas for new strategies that might be helpful. Provide extra sheets of Appendix B and paper in case students want to add on to their work from yesterday. Confer as you did yesterday, supporting students further to develop strategies and big ideas described in the Overview and depicted on the landscape.

Facilitating the Gallery Walk

Have students display their posters in the classroom for other groups to view. If you have used drawing paper, you can display the posters around the room or on tables. Posters might also be displayed on easels or taped to a whiteboard. Once all the groups have placed their posters up for display, explain to your students that during a gallery walk they will walk around and look at the other posters. They will have an important job: reading to try to understand what another group was showing on their poster. Explain to students that they will walk silently around reading the posters. As they walk around they should be thinking about questions like, "Do I understand this?" "Is this like what I did on my poster?" "Is this an arrangement I found, too?" "Am I confused about a part?" and "Do I disagree?"

Give your students sticky notes so that they can share their reactions to each poster. You may wish to give your students blank post-it notes so that they can draw or write their ideas, or you may wish to provide them with the following pre-made sticky notes:

> ✓ **Check Mark:** I really understand this.
> ? **Question Mark:** I wonder about this, or I have a question here.
> **Connection sign:** I agree. I did the same thing on my poster.

Have students walk around and read a few of the posters silently for 5-10 minutes. Tell them they do not have to read every poster. It is best that they really spend time on only a few instead of trying to look at all of them superficially. Just make sure that every poster gets read by a least a few children and that every poster gets at least a few sticky notes.

After the gallery walk, invite the groups to go back to their posters to see what comments were left. By having this gallery walk, you are encouraging your students to reflect and comment on written and visual forms of mathematics—something professional mathematicians do! They are learning to write and read a viable argument, one of the CCSS Standards of Mathematical Practice.

Facilitating the Math Congress

Gather the students together in a meeting area and carefully choose a few posters for discussion that will foster a conversation on several powerful ideas from the landscape such as commutativity and/or compensation and associativity. The intent of the congress is to promote a discussion on ways to determine equivalent arrangements.

Inside One Classroom: A Portion of the Math Congress

Anna (the teacher): Jade and Maya, would you bring your poster up here and talk about the big thing you noticed as you worked?

Jade: We made lots of ways with ones. See, we wrote 1+1+1+1+1 = 5. Then we made that into 3+2 by putting some together.

Anna: Who knows what Jade and Maya did? Show with a connection sign if you agree. Harrison, can you explain in your words what they did?

Harrison: I think they just moved chicks around.

Anna: Turn to your neighbor and discuss this. How are Jade and Maya moving the chicks? *(After a few moments of pair talk, Anna resumes conversation. She uses the 5-bead Mathrack™ to represent the quantities during the discussion.)* So, they started with 5 ones. These were like the 5 chicks. I'll move the beads over to show the 5 chicks. How did they make 3+2 from that? Do you want to keep going Harrison?

Harrison: They put two together.

Anna: Like this? *(She moves two beads a bit to the right, leaving a group of three on the left.)* Is this still 5? Does their strategy work? Turn to an elbow partner and talk about this. *(After a moment, Anna calls on Tanika.)*

Tanika: It does work. They are just moving the chicks, but it is still 5.

Chad: Yep. It's still 5 chicks. They are all there. The wolf didn't take any.

Anna: So, if we just move some around it doesn't change how many there are? We don't even need to count? It is still 5? Can we move another chick over? *(Anna moves one more bead to the right and now 2+3 is shown.)*

Owen: Hey, wow! That's a good way, Jade. I see another way. Move one more over. Now we have 1+4, but it is still 5.

Anna: This is a great strategy, Jade and Maya. We'll name it after you and put it up on our strategy wall.

Author's notes

Anna focuses discussion here on some big ideas. She chooses this piece of work because it will support her community to consider and construct conservation, compensation, and associativity.

By providing time for reflection and a consideration of whether the ideas work to make an equivalent arrangement, Anna gets the community engaged. She does not end up in a dialogue with only Jade and Maya.

Now Anna challenges children to consider how counting may not be necessary. The amount is conserved if nothing has been removed. Even if the arrangements look different, they are equivalent.

Notice how the students are given credit for the invention of the strategy. They are young mathematicians at work and they have justified that amounts can be rearranged and still be equivalent.

Reflections on the Day

It is only the second day of the unit, but you have probably already witnessed movement along the landscape of learning. It is important to document this growth for each child. Movement on the landscape is about genuine mathematics development. This is a much deeper, more powerful and genuine way to do formative assessment than to think of lessons having just one objective that everyone is supposed to "get." Some teachers copy the graphic of the landscape and use a yellow highlighter to trace individual pathways for each child to produce data for documentation of learning. Samples of children's work can be placed in portfolios and dated as samples. New Perspectives on Assessment (www.NewPerspectivesOnAssessment.com) also provides an app that allows you to do this record-keeping digitally and to take photos of children's work with a cell phone or tablet and attach them to the graphic.

DAY THREE

FINDING FIVE CHICKS

Materials Needed
Quick Images Cards (Appendix C)
Class-size 5-bead Mathrack™
Individual 5-bead Mathracks™ (one per group of four students)
Cards for the game *Finding Five Chicks* (Appendix E, one set per group of four students)
Several sheets of copy paper and pencils for each group

Today begins with a minilesson using the set of quick images from Appendix C. The set of images is designed to support the development of compensation and associativity and once again the 5-bead Mathrack™ is used to represent students' strategies during discussion. Afterwards, students are introduced to a new game: *Finding Five Chicks.* They play two or three rounds in groups of four, each time recording the matches they make that show all five of Rhoda's chicks, and working to achieve a higher score than their score in previous rounds.

Day Three Outline

Minilesson: A String of Related Problems
❖ Use the same set of quick images used yesterday (provided in Appendix C), but in a different order. Show one image at a time and invite discussion of strategies.
❖ Use the class-size 5-bead Mathrack™ to represent student strategies.

Developing the Context
❖ Remind students of the story *Are You All Here?* and then introduce the game *Finding Five Chicks*.

Supporting the Investigation
❖ Students work in groups of four playing *Finding Five Chicks*. Provide each group with a set of cards and blank paper and pencils for recording matches that make 5.
❖ Confer with students as they play, supporting the development of strategies and big ideas from the landscape in the Overview.

Minilesson: A String of Related Problems

Use the set of quick image cards provided on Appendix C. Show one image at a time in the order below **(note that this order is different than the order you used yesterday)** and invite students to determine how many chicks are on the cards. As strategies are shared for determining the total of the chicks, use the class-size 5-bead Mathrack™ to represent student thinking. To represent compensation and associativity, move one bead over slowly to support children to see the equivalence and write the two expressions as an equation, as illustrated below and in the following dialogue box.

The String:
    1+4
    2+3
    3+2
    4+1
  5 on the left

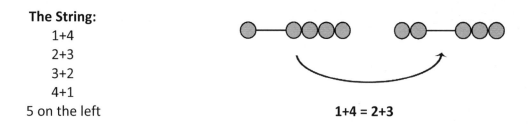

1+4 = 2+3

Teacher Note

The string is designed to support the development of compensation and associativity. However, do not describe or ask students to use this strategy. Just use the cards, supporting discussion and accepting and representing on the mathrack all strategies that students offer. Equivalence will naturally arise because no matter what strategies children use the answers will be the same. Invite students to consider why this is and let them feel like they have invented the idea. At this young age the formal name *associative property* is not necessary. Children often name it "give and take" or they say, "just move one [or some] over." Name the strategy after the child who first offers and justifies it and post it on the strategy wall with an example. To jazz up and personalize your strategy wall, you can post pictures of your young mathematicians and use conversation bubbles with examples of their insights.

Inside One Classroom: A Portion of the Minilesson

Anna (the teacher): Here is our first one. It is going by quickly so make sure you are looking! *(Shows 1+4.)* Ok, thumbs up when you are ready to share how many chicks you saw. *(When most thumbs are up, Anna starts discussion.)*

Jodi: I saw 5. I know because I counted: 1, 2, 3, 4, 5.

Anna: *(Using the Mathrack™)* Like this? You saw 1 chick and said "1", and then added on saying "2, 3, 4, 5"? *(She shows the quick image again so children can check and writes "1+4 = 5.")* Did anyone do it a different way? Elsa?

Elsa: I started with the 4. It was faster. I just said in my mind that 1 more was 5.

Anna: Wow! That was fast, and I think you used Jade's idea from yesterday? I put it up on our strategy wall. She called it "the switch-a-roo" and said, "when you add it doesn't matter which number you do first." *(Anna points to the strategy wall and flips the math rack to show the commutative property.)* I think instead of doing 1+4, you did 4+1? I'm going to write your thinking like this: 1+4 = 4+1. Ok, here's the next one *(shows 2+3)*. Don't forget to show me with a thumb when you are ready. *(Noticing that several students are counting, Anna decides to have pair talk.)* Turn and talk to your elbow partner. *(After a few minutes, she resumes whole group discussion.)* Did anyone have an interesting partner who tried a really fast way?

Maya: *(Counting by ones to check what her partner has said.)* Hannah said it was the same as 1+4. I checked, and it is.

Hannah: One chick just moved. You had 1 chick here and 4 over there. Now it is 2 here and only 3 over there because a chick moved over.

Anna: One chick just went to the other group? Are the 5 chicks still all there? Is Hannah right, Maya? If we just move chicks from one group to another it is still 5? We don't need to count? Wow, that is a fast way! *(Using the mathrack, Anna sets up 1+4, then moves a bead from the right to the left, effectively turning 1+4 into 2+3.)*

Maya: Yes. They are all there. I just moved one over in my mind. It's like what Jade and I did yesterday!

Anna: Wow. This is a great strategy! We'll get this strategy up on the strategy wall, too! Jade, Maya, and Hannah's "move around rule."

Author's notes

Anna accepts all strategies and models them on the Mathrack™. She does not explain strategies first; she lets them emerge in the discussion. The way the string is crafted will support development.

The Mathrack™ is a helpful tool for thinking. Anna also represents the equivalence using an equation. Many children think the equal sign means the answer is coming. Anna writes an equation to ensure her students develop an understanding of the equal sign as a symbol to show equivalence.

Anna celebrates the emergence of the associative property and declares a new jointly authored strategy for the wall display.

Developing the Context

After the minilesson, ask students to form a circle. Invite one child into the center with you and demonstrate how to play the game *Finding Five Chicks*. The game is played like Concentration. All 16 cards (from Appendix E) are turned over face down in 4 rows of 4. Directions follow:

Finding Five Chicks

Set-up: All cards of the chicks are laid out face down in the center of the playing area in an array, 4 rows of 4.

Objective: To make matches showing all 5 of Rhoda's chicks.

Game Play:

❖ Play is cooperative as players work to make as many groups of 5 as they can.

❖ Players take turns turning over one card and laying it face up. If it is a match with another face-up card to make all 5 of Rhoda's chicks (**looking carefully to make sure there aren't duplicates of the same chick—5 different chicks are needed**), the matching cards are removed from the center and placed face-up in a row next to each other.

❖ Players continue taking turns picking a card and together they make as many matches as possible.

Once children understand how to play, form groups of four students and provide materials to each group: a set of cards, a Mathrack™, a sheet of paper, and a pencil. Ask them to play two or three rounds and keep track of the matches they find, trying to beat their earlier scores.

Teacher Note

Many teachers find it helpful to use cardstock and laminate the cards. Although this is time consuming the first time you make your sets, they will be durable, and you'll never have to make them again. If you want to really jazz them up, you can use rolls of contact paper or wallpaper to achieve colorful backs. Clear contact plastic can also be used in place of lamination. It can often be found in Dollar stores. Manila folders can also be used to organize your games. Small resealable plastic baggies can be used to hold the cards and other playing pieces and can be stapled to the inside of the folder to keep small parts from being lost. The directions can also be stapled on the inside. (The directions are provided in Appendix D if you wish to do this.) The name of the game can be written on the tab and multiple copies can be placed together in a milk carton crate. Although children will not likely be able to read the directions, if you have assistant or push-in teachers, or volunteering parents, you can just hand the folder to them and they can immediately work with a group without you taking time to explain what to do. This is also a helpful organization scheme for substitute and student teachers.

Supporting the Investigation

It is likely that children initially will group in a variety of ways. For example, they may make 5 with 2+2+1. Doing so will result in cards left on the table that cannot be matched. The cards are designed with size as a support, so even though students can't see the number of chicks until a card is turned over, they may begin to use the size of the card as a clue to find a missing addend. The more they can do this, the higher the likelihood of having no cards left at the end. This will happen when they consistently make matches with only two addends: 3+2; 2+3; 1+4; or 4+1.

As children play, move around and confer. At some point, it may be helpful to ask children to justify the commutative property. For example, they will likely produce: 3+2 = 2+3, and 1+4 = 4+1. Encourage them to justify why order doesn't matter. After a few rounds, some children may notice that really there are only two ways to make 5 that they need to search for: 3+2 and 1+4. Realizing this and using size as a support to find the required cards will result in eight matches with no cards left on the table. Thus, this is the highest score possible. Don't be too directive in conferring. Let the ideas emerge during play.

Reflections on the Day

Math workshop began today again with a minilesson where students were encouraged to discuss conservation, equivalence, associativity, and compensation. Then they were introduced to a new game: *Finding Five Chicks.* The game supported them to revisit commutativity. Realizing that they only need to remember and search for two expressions as ways to make 5 will provide students a powerful foundation for prioritizing the 5-structure. You are witnessing major development in front of your eyes and it is important to document it. Review the landscape in the overview. Have you seen your children traversing the landscape? Continue to document each child's journey. You can highlight each child's path on the graphic of the landscape provided in the overview of this unit. Remember that there is also an app available if you wish to capture and document your students' development digitally. The app, available at www.NewPerspectivesOnAssessment.com, allows you to make short video clips as children play.

DAY FOUR

FISH FOR FIVES

Materials Needed

Class-size 5-bead Mathrack™

Individual 5-bead Mathracks™ (one per group of four students)

Cards for the game *Fish for Fives* (Appendix G, one set per group of four students)

Several sheets of copy paper and pencils for each group

Today begins with another minilesson, this time using a string of related addition and subtraction problems. The string is designed to support the prioritizing of the 5-structure by developing an understanding of the relationship between addition and subtraction and the part/whole relations within five. Once again, the 5-bead Mathrack™ is used to represent students' strategies during discussion. Afterwards students are introduced to another new game: *Fish for Fives.*

Day Four Outline

Minilesson: A String of Related Problems

❖ Show one problem at a time from a string of related addition and subtraction problems and invite discussion of strategies.

❖ Use the class-size 5-bead Mathrack™ to represent student strategies.

Developing the Context

❖ Introduce the game *Fish for Fives.*

Supporting the Investigation

❖ Students work in groups of four playing *Fish for Fives.* Provide each group with a set of cards and blank paper and pencils for recording matches.

❖ Confer with students as they play, supporting the development of strategies and big ideas from the landscape described in the Overview.

Minilesson: A String of Related Problems

Show one problem at a time from the string of problems below. As students share their strategies for determining the answer, use the 5-bead class-size Mathrack™ to represent each student's thinking.

The String

1+4

5 − 1

5 − 4

2+3

3+2

5 − 2

5 − 3

Inside One Classroom: A Portion of the Minilesson	
Anna (the teacher): Here is our first one. *(Writes,"1+4.")* Ok, thumbs up when you are ready to share. *(When most thumbs are up, Anna starts discussion.)* **Jodi:** It's 5. I know because… I just remember that one. **Anna:** *(Using the Mathrack, Anna first pushes 1 bead to the left, and then moves the remaining 4 to the left as well, in one move as a group.)* Like this? Here is 1 and you just knew 4 more would be 5. It's helpful when you just know, isn't it? Did anyone do it a different way? Eli? **Eli:** I started with the 4. I just knew that 1 more would make 5. **Anna:** Wow! The old "switch-a-roo" again. That's a popular strategy. I think instead of doing 1+4, you did 4+1? I'm going to write your thinking like this: 1+4 = 4+1. Ok, here's the next one. *(She writes "5 − 1.")* Don't forget to show me with a thumb when you are ready. **Maya:** I used what Eli said. For the last problem, he said he added 1 onto 4. So, if we take 1 away from 5, we are back to 4. **Anna:** Oh, that is very interesting, Maya. You are talking about how addition and subtraction are related. Everyone, turn and talk to the person next to you about what Maya did. How are addition and subtraction related? *(Anna waits a few minutes and listens in on a few conversations.)* Jake and Jade, would you tell us what you talked about? **Jake:** *(Holds up 5 fingers, then pushes the thumb down.)* See, 4+1, but then if I push the thumb down I have 4.	 *Author's notes* *Anna accepts that some of the facts are now becoming automatic. "I just know that one," is a comment to be celebrated. No further explanation is necessary as the relations can be modeled on the Mathrack. Often teachers require explanation. But, doing so when a child has automatized the fact can be detrimental. Trying to please the teacher, the child often reverts to explaining counting to justify the answer, when that wasn't the strategy used at all.*

Anna: Come stand up here Jake and show the kids what you are doing with your fingers. I'll model it on the Mathrack™. *(Anna starts with 5 beads on the left and then slides the fifth bead over to the right and then back to the left as Jake talks about his thumb.)* Wow, that is a nice connection. We can see the addition and the subtraction. I wonder if that idea would be helpful for this one? *(Anna writes "5 – 4" and several students start using their fingers to count backwards.)*

Maya: I think it is the same.

Anna: What do you mean, Maya. How is it the same? The same as what?

Maya: 4+1 is 5, so if you start with 5 and take 4 away, you have 1 left. *(Representing Maya's thinking, Anna shows 5 beads first on the left, then moves a group of 4 to the right, leaving 1 on the left.)*

The Mathrack™ is a helpful tool for thinking. Anna uses it here as a representational tool to illustrate the relations under discussion.

Anna probes for clarification and then represents Maya's thinking on the 5-bead Mathrack™.

Developing the Context

After the minilesson, ask students to form a circle. Invite one child into the center with you and demonstrate how to play the game *Fish for Fives*. Directions for making the cards and for playing can be found on Appendix G. Directions for playing are also shown below:

Fish for Fives

Set-up: All cards are placed in a face-down pile in the center of the playing area and each player chooses one card from the pile.

Objective: To match players' cards into equations that equal 5.

Game Play:

❖ One at a time, each player asks the group for the card he needs to make a total of 5 with the card in his hand. [For example, if the first player has a 3, he would ask the group if anyone has a 2.]

❖ If no one has the requested card, the asking player must choose a second card from the deck. If another player does have the number requested, she gives it to the requestor. If this player is left with no cards in her hand, she then chooses another card from the deck, but she has to wait until her next turn to use it.

❖ If the requestor received a card, the matching two cards are placed face up, so everyone can see the match that makes 5. If the match is not a correct one, the player keeps both cards, and the player to the left now becomes a requestor. If everyone agrees the match is a correct one and can justify that the total is 5 (a match), the requestor writes the equation on the recording sheet. [For example, he would write "3+2 = 5."] Then he completes his turn by taking another card from the deck.

❖ Play continues like this unless a 5 or a joker is drawn. Whenever a 5 is drawn, the player takes some little squares (1-4, player's choice) out of the envelope and covers up a corresponding amount on the 5. The remaining amount becomes the card requested, and a smart move is to make a card in the player's hand usable. [For example, if a player uses 3 squares to cover 3 hearts, she requests a 2, but if the player has a 2 in her hand she can use it instead of requesting from the other players.] If a 2 is produced, the equation written is 5 – 3 = 2. If no one has a 2, a card is drawn from the deck and the turn passes to the next player.

❖ When a joker is drawn, it can be used for any number needed, but the player must justify why that number works.

❖ The group's score is the number of equations they have made when all cards from the deck have been drawn.

Once children understand how to play, form groups of four students and provide materials to each group: a set of cards, a 5-bead Mathrack™, a sheet of paper, and a pencil.

Teacher Note

The set of cards for *Fish for Fives* is provided in Appendix G. However, many teachers find it more useful to make their own sets out of decks of playing cards as they are more durable. Directions follow for making the set of cards from a deck of playing cards if you wish to do so.

Remove all cards marked 2, 3, 4, and 5 from a deck of playing cards, as well as the four aces and the jokers. These are the only cards you will be using. With a pair of scissors, cut out the extra suit images under the numerals. Doing so ensures that children see a set of objects that correctly matches the numerals on the cards. Save all the small squares that you cut out and place them in a resealable plastic baggie. Cut small squares out of the jokers as well, so that players cannot tell jokers when the cards are face down. With the aces, place a sticky circle over the A and write the numeral 1 on it. The picture below shows the resulting cards. There should be 20 cards in all, plus the jokers. Store all cards and the small squares in the plastic baggie.

Figure 4. Playing Cards Adapted to Play *Fish for Fives*.

Supporting the Investigation

As children play, move around and confer. Note the strategies children use to find the missing addend. Do they count on, count backwards, or do they just know the fact? There really are only two facts that need to be automatic: 2+3 and 1+ 4. The commutative property produces the other two combinations. At this point in the unit, several students will likely know these two facts. But, there may still be some children who are still relying on counting strategies. As they play, encourage them to use the Mathrack™ at the table for support.

Reflections on the Day

Math workshop began today again with a minilesson where students were encouraged to explore the relation between addition and subtraction. Then they were introduced to a new game: *Fish for Fives.* The game supported them to continue exploring addition and subtraction. Tomorrow a third game will be introduced for further support in encouraging the prioritizing of the 5-structure. In kindergarten, games are an integral part of math workshop. Games can be used throughout the year and provide a powerful tool for differentiation. Many of the schools using CFLM also use DreamBox. During math workshop it is a common practice to have children working in small groups playing different games and/or working on computers using DreamBox.

DAY FIVE

HOW MANY ARE HIDING?

Materials Needed

Sets of materials in small plastic bags for *Building Equations* (Prepared dice and cards from Appendix I, one set for each group of four students)

Individual 5-bead Mathracks™ (one per group of four students)

Pencils and sheets of copy or drawing paper to use as a scorecard

Today begins with another minilesson designed to support the development of the structure of five. Using the 5-bead Mathrack™, quick images of various parts of the group of 5 are shown and students are asked to determine how many beads are covered. Afterwards they learn a new game, *Building Equations,* which they play with Mathrack™ cards and dice.

Day Five Outline

Minilesson: A String of Related Problems
❖ Use the 5-bead Mathrack™ to work on a string of related missing addend problems.

Developing the Context
❖ Introduce the game *Building Equations.*

Supporting the Investigation
❖ Confer with children as they work, noting the strategies they use to find the matching piece.

Minilesson: A String of Related Problems

This string is designed to support the use of known addition facts to determine missing addends. The part/whole relations within five are still the focus. Use the class-size 5-bead Mathrack™ to create one image at a time from the string of problems below, asking students to determine how many beads are under your hand. As strategies are shared for determining the answer, use the Mathrack™ to represent student thinking.

The String

Show 4 beads on the left side and cover the 1 remaining on the right, asking, "How many are hiding?"

1 shown, 4 hidden
4 shown, 1 hidden
3 shown, 2 hidden
2 shown, 3 hidden
5 shown, 0 hidden—but pretend you have some hidden

Inside One Classroom: A Portion of the Minilesson

Anna (the teacher): Here is our first one. *(Shows 4, with the 1 remaining hidden in her fist.)* How many are hiding? Thumbs up when you are ready to share. *(When most thumbs are up, Anna starts discussion.)*

Jodi: It's 1. I know because… 1 more is 5. I just remember that one.

Anna: *(Using the* Mathrack™ *Anna opens her fist, shows the bead hidden in it, and moves it to the left to make 5.)* It's helpful when you just know, isn't it? Did anyone do it a different way? Ella?

Ella: I started with the 4. I just knew that one more would make 5.

Anna: Ok, here's the next one *(shows 1 and covers 4)*. Don't forget to show me with a thumb when you are ready.

Janet: I used what Ella said. I started with 1 and counted on with my fingers. It's 4, see? *(She holds up her fingers.)*

Anna: Julian?

Julian: I used the "switch-a-roo." Instead of doing 1+4, I did 4+1.

Anna: I'm going to write your thinking like this: 1+4 = 4+1. Jake?

Jake: *(Holds up 5 fingers, and points to his thumb.)* I agree with Julian. See, 1+4, but then if I push the thumb down I have 4 and that's 4+1.

Author's notes

The Mathrack™ is a helpful tool for thinking. Anna uses it here as a representational tool to illustrate the relations under discussion. Note that she also writes an equation as children are now quite comfortable talking about equations. The Mathrack™ and the activities in this first week of the unit have supported children to move away from counting strategies. They are now using a network of relations.

Developing the Context

After the minilesson, ask students to form a circle. Invite one child into the center with you and demonstrate how to play the game *Building Equations*. The cards for playing can be found on Appendix I. Directions for playing follow:

Building Equations

Set-up: All cards are placed face-up in the middle of the table. Players will also use a 6-sided die in which the 6 has been covered by a white dot or other obscuring sticker.

Objective: To build and capture expressions equivalent to 5.

Game Play:

❖ During the first round, each player takes a turn to roll the die and a card that matches it. [For example, if a player rolls a 4, she chooses a card with 4 beads on it and places it face-up in front of her. If the white dot is rolled, the player may choose any number.] Now all players each have one card.

❖ On the second and later rounds, the roll of the die may produce a card that makes a total of 5 when placed with one of the player's existing cards. If this is the case, the player gets to take a plus sign and builds an expression that is equal to 5. [For example, at this point a player might have 3+2, if he already had a 3 and he just rolled a 2.]

❖ Play continues in turns with players building expressions equivalent to 5 when they can. If at any point a player rolls a 5, she takes a 5-card from the table and uses it to capture an equivalent expression from the table. The player puts the expression in the envelope, recording the equation on the group's scorecard, then places the 5-card back on the table. [If she captured 3+2, she would write 3+2 = 5, and would place the 3 and 2 cards in the envelope and the 5-card back on the table.]

❖ When the die rolled has a blank face (white dot), a player can use it to be any number he needs. [He might want it to be a 5 so he can capture an equivalent expression, or he might want it to serve for a missing addend, so he can make an expression and take a plus sign.]

❖ The objective is to get all the 1-4 cards back in the envelope. The group's final score is the number of equations they build.

Once children understand how to play, form groups of four students and provide materials to each group: a set of cards and a die, a 5-bead Mathrack™, a sheet of paper, and a pencil.

Supporting the Investigation

As children play, move around and confer. As with *Fish for Fives*, note the strategies children use to find the missing addend. Do they count on, count backwards, or do they just know the fact? There really are only two facts that need to be automatic: 2+3 and 1+ 4. The commutative property produces the other two combinations. At this point in the unit, several students will likely know these two facts. But, there may still be some children who are still relying on counting strategies. As they play, encourage them to use the Mathrack™ at the table for support and to move away from counting.

Reflections on the Day

Math workshop began today again with a minilesson where students were encouraged to explore missing addends. Then they were introduced to a new game: *Building Equations.* The game supported them to continue exploring strategies for determining missing addends. As you complete the first week of this unit, note which children now easily see 5 as a set that is composed of and can be decomposed into subitizable units of 1, 2, 3, and 4. If some of your children are still counting to ensure they have 5, continue to work with them using quick images. It is important to support them in developing a strong understanding of the 5-structure, without needing to count, as next week the 10-structure will be the focus.

DAY SIX

IS THE GANG OF TEN ALL HERE?

Materials Needed

The Gang's All Here
[A full-color read-aloud is available from Amazon.com. If you do not have it, you can use Appendix J]

Class-size 10-bead Mathrack™
(available from www.Mathrack.com)

Individual 10-bead Mathracks™ (one per pair of students, available from www.Mathrack.com)

Drawing paper and markers or pencils

Glue sticks and scissors, one each per pair of students

The 10 Chicks
(Appendix K, several sets per pair)

The story *The Gang's All Here* sets the stage for investigating various arrangements of 10 chicks playing in the barnyard as their anxious mothers try to make sure none of the chicks have been eaten by the fox. Rhoda's friend Loretta has now given birth to 5 chicks and Rhoda's chicks take them out to the barnyard to show them around. After the children hear the story and act it out on the 10-bead Mathrack™, they go off to investigate finding, and recording, various possible arrangements of the 10 chicks. The 10-bead Mathrack™ and the baby chick context are introduced and used to support the development of equivalence and compensation; for example, the situation of 6 chicks on the left and 4 chicks on the right side of the barnyard is explored as being equivalent to 5 chicks on the left and 5 chicks on the right. One chick has just moved. Now that the 5-structure has been developed, the second week of the unit is designed to build the part/whole relations of the 10-structure.

Day Six Outline

Developing the Context
❖ Read the story *The Gang's All Here*.
❖ Introduce the 10-bead Mathrack™ and help children use it to act out the story.

Supporting the Investigation
❖ Note children's strategies as they explore different ways the chicks might be arranged in the barnyard. Confer by celebrating their attempts and challenging them to find other equivalent arrangements.

Developing the Context

Read *The Gang's All Here* (Appendix J). Allow children to discuss their ideas about whether all the chicks are in the barnyard as you are reading the story. The purpose of the reading is to draw children's attention to the idea that Rhoda's and Loretta's chicks (5+5) can be arranged in ways that look very different but that are still the same 10 chicks.

Introduce the 10-bead Mathrack™, using it to model the situations in the read-aloud. Note the similarity of the colors of the chicks to the beads on the rack and ask the children how they think  it might look if you used the rack to retell and act out some of the puzzling moments in the story. Make sure students agree that the 10 beads can be used to represent the 10 chicks. This assumption requires 1-1 correspondence and for those who have yet to construct this idea it may not be apparent.

As you retell the story, ask children to share how they know the chicks are still all there in each scenario. Use the 10-bead Mathrack™ to model children's strategies as they share. For example, if a child counts, move one bead at a time as he counts. However, remind the children of what they know from the first week of this unit and move all the red beads as a group as you remind them. If a child counts on, slide the group she starts with over with one push, also treating it as a group, and then count on. If a child uses the commutative property, turn the rack over to show how order does not matter (commutativity). If a child says, 6+4 is equal to 5+5 because one of the chicks just moved, show 5 beads on the left and 5 beads on the right and then slowly move a bead from the right to the left to produce 6+4 (compensation and associativity).

After a discussion about a few of the students' favorite moments where the chicks were playing tricks on their mother, remind children of what they did on Day One of the unit and that they have made you curious now about how many ways the 10 chicks can group themselves to fool their mothers. Suggest they work with a partner to investigate and see if they can figure out ways the chicks could fool their mother by being in different groups, but still being 10 altogether. Invite them to tell their own stories of different ways the 10 chicks can arrange themselves. Pass out copies of Appendix K, glue sticks, pencils (or markers), 10-racks, and scissors. Have students cut out groups of chicks from the Appendix and glue them onto the paper. Remind them that Rhoda only has 5 chicks and Loretta only has 5 chicks, so they will need to think about how many of each they cut out. Support them to write stories and equations on their drawings and to model the action on an individual 10-bead Mathrack™ with their math partner. [Note: You can give students larger drawing paper or several sheets of 8.5 x 11 paper to illustrate their ideas. If you use drawing paper, they will likely be able to do several arrangements on one piece. If you use 8.5 x 11 copy paper, have them do one arrangement on each piece. These can then be stapled together into a book for each child to take home.]

Supporting the Investigation

As students begin to work, make a quick scan of the room to make sure all students are engaged. If some students are not engaged, check first to make sure they understand the context. With partners who are not clear about what to do, you might suggest that they take turns visualizing an arrangement of the chicks that Rhoda and Loretta might see in the barnyard and show it to their partner on the 10-bead Mathrack™. Suggest that it can be hard to remember all the arrangements they might come up with, so they will need to show each of the arrangements they make on their drawing paper. Or, have them make up their own stories of what might be going on in the barnyard. Provide multiple copies of the strips of the chicks and explain that you have extra copies as well if they need more. Once a partnership agrees on an arrangement that might fool Rhoda and Loretta, they should cut out the chicks from the corresponding strips to match their groupings and arrange and paste them on the drawing paper. For children who are ready to write numerals, you can encourage them to write their story in a math statement: for example, if they have started with 5+5 and had a chick leave the group and go over to the group of chicks on the other side, thereby making 4+6, you might encourage them to write: "5+5 = 4+6."

Once most students are fully engaged, take note of the strategies you see and choose a few pairs to sit and confer with. You will likely see several strategies as you did on Days One and Two when children decomposed five. Look over the landscape in the Overview. As children work, listen for the big ideas and strategies and support children to think about them. Remember as you confer to clarify first what learners are doing. Once clarification is achieved, the conferral is characterized by cycles of celebrating and challenging.

Reflections on the Day

Today, children were introduced to the 10-bead Mathrack™. Within the context of baby chicks moving around in the barnyard, they explored conservation, compensation, equivalence, and cardinality. On Day Seven they will have opportunities to continue the work and a congress will be held providing for a discussion on some of the big ideas that emerged.

DAY SEVEN

EQUIVALENCE REVISITED

Materials Needed

The Gang's All Here
[A full-color read-aloud is available from Amazon.com. If you do not have it, you can use Appendix J]

Class-size 10-bead Mathrack™

Individual 10-bead Mathracks™ (one per pair of students)

Pencils

Students' work from Day Six

Several sheets of copy or drawing paper and markers or pencils

Glue sticks, one per pair of students

Scissors, one per pair of students

The 10 Chicks
(Appendix K, several extra sets)

Today begins again with a minilesson as a warm-up to math workshop. As on Day Two, students work with a string of related images designed to support the development of the commutative property, but this time using expressions that equal 10. After the minilesson, students are given an opportunity to revisit their thinking from Day Six, and to revise or add on to their work in preparation for a gallery walk and math congress. The focus of the congress is equivalence of expressions that make 10.

Day Seven Outline

Minilesson: A String of Related Problems
❖ Use the string of problems to do quick images on the class-size 10-bead Mathrack™. Show one at a time and invite discussion of strategies.

Supporting the Investigation:
❖ Remind students of the story *The Gang's All Here* and provide students with time to revisit their work from yesterday and to revise as they wish in preparation of a gallery walk and math congress.

Facilitating the Gallery Walk
❖ Post student work around the room and invite review.

Facilitating the Math Congress
❖ Invite two or three pairs to share their work to the group.
❖ Foster discussion on some big ideas from the landscape that emerged related to equivalence, for example commutativity or compensation and associativity. Use the class-size 10-bead Mathrack™ to model the strategies and big ideas during the discussion.

Minilesson: A String of Related Problems

Work through the string of related problems showing one at a time on the mathrack. Arrange them behind your back, or cover them with a screen or cloth, then flash as a quick image for a few seconds, then cover again, inviting discussion on how many were shown in all. As strategies are shared for determining the total of the beads, move the beads accordingly on the Mathrack™ to represent student thinking. For example, if a student says, "6+4 is the same as 5+5, a white bead just moved over," move the bead slowly to show the change being described. Doing so supports your students to construct compensation and associativity.

The String:
5 red on the left and 5 white on the right
6 on the left and 4 on the right
7 on the left and 3 on the right
3 on the left and 7 on the right
4 on the left and 6 on the right
10 on the left

Teacher Note

The string is designed to support the development of several big ideas on the landscape: compensation, associativity, and commutativity. These ideas were the focus throughout week one as well, but don't be surprised if some children are challenged with these ideas now that you have moved to 10 beads. They may have been helped in week one by the fact that the smaller groups could be subitized. This week they will need to generalize the ideas beyond the small subitizable groups.

Remember to build a strategy wall to display all the "inventions" children have discovered and justified and add to it throughout the year. Having a wall of strategies on display allows children to revisit, reflect, and use previously justified ideas and strategies. If commutativity and associativity are up on the wall from the work in week one, point to them and exclaim how wonderful it is that some of the ideas invented last week can be used with big numbers too!

Supporting the Investigation

Remind students of the story *The Gang's All Here*. Explain that the class will have a gallery walk to look at each other's work from Day Six but that you want to provide time first in case anyone wants to add on to what they did yesterday, revise, or write about strategies they discovered. Suggest that the minilesson might even have provided ideas for new strategies that might be helpful. Provide extra sheets of Appendix K and paper in case students want to add on to their work from yesterday. Confer as you did yesterday, but today also encourage students to determine if they have found all the ways and to work to defend how they know. Don't expect all your students to be able to work systematically, but be alert for those you can support to do so. For example, some may begin to use compensation and encouraging these students to make a list and use it consistently may result in a systematic approach: 9+1 = 8+2 = 7+3 = 6+4, etc.

Facilitating the Gallery Walk

As you did on Day Two, have students display their posters in the classroom for other groups to view. If you have used drawing paper, you can display the posters around the room or on tables. Others can be displayed on easels or taped to a whiteboard. Once all the groups have placed their posters up for display, remind your students that during a gallery walk they will walk around and look at the other posters and that this is a silent time so everyone can read and write helpful comments.

Give your students sticky notes so that they can share their reactions to each poster. For others challenged by writing, you may wish to provide them with the following pre-made sticky notes:

- ✓ **Check Mark:** I really understand this.
- ? **Question Mark:** I wonder about this, or I have a question here.
- ⇄ **Connection sign:** I agree. I did the same thing on my poster.

Have students walk around and read a few of the posters silently for 5-10 minutes. Tell them they do not have to read every poster. It is best that they really spend time on only a few instead of trying to look at all of them superficially. Just make sure that every poster gets read by at least a few children and that every poster gets at least a few sticky notes.

After the gallery walk, invite the groups to go back to their posters to see what comments were left. By having this gallery walk, you are encouraging your students to reflect and comment on written and visual forms of mathematics—something professional mathematicians do! They are learning to write and read a viable argument, one of the CCSS Standards of Mathematical Practice.

Facilitating the Math Congress

Gather the students together in a meeting area and carefully choose a few posters for discussion that will foster a conversation on a few powerful ideas from the landscape such as commutativity and/or compensation and associativity. The intent of the congress is to promote a discussion on ways to determine equivalent arrangements.

Inside One Classroom: A Portion of the Math Congress

Anna (the teacher): Ella and Hope, would you bring your poster up here and talk about the big thing you noticed as you worked? You found that the switch-a-roo that you used last week worked for these bigger numbers too, didn't you?

Ella: Yes. We did 6+4 and then we switched it around and did 4+6. Then we did 7+3 and switched that one around, too! We made lots of ways by switching.

Anna: Who knows what Ella means? Show with a connection sign if you agree. *(She sees lots of connecting signs.)* So, are we saying that whenever we add we can just switch the numbers and the total will still be the same? Wow! This is a big idea that will save a lot of work. We don't have to count? Turn to your neighbor and discuss this.

(Anna pauses for a moment and speaks again when the conversation begins to die down.)

Anna: This is a great strategy, girls! We'll name it after you and put it up on our strategy wall.

Author's notes

Anna chooses this piece of work because it will support her community to consider and construct the commutative property for addition.

By providing time for reflection and a consideration of whether the ideas work to make equivalent arrangement, Anna gets the community engaged. She does not end up in a dialogue with only Ella.

Strategies are named after the mathematicians who justify them, and they go up on a strategy wall for reflection and use over the year.

Reflections on the Day

Now that you are working with 10, you are probably noticing how the big ideas that students developed in week one are now being generalized. Many children are probably also making use of a group of 5— they are prioritizing it, not counting each bead but moving the group on the Mathrack™ all at once. It is important to document this growth for each child. Movement on the landscape is about genuine mathematical development. As mentioned earlier in the unit, this is a much deeper, more powerful way to do formative assessment than to think of lessons as having just one objective that everyone is supposed to "get." Mark the growth on the graphic of the landscape and trace individual pathways for each child to produce data for documentation of learning. Or, use your app and take pictures of students' work or short videos of kids talking about big ideas (www.NewPerspectivesOnAssessment.com) and attach them to the digital landscape graphic to make entries about what you are noticing.

DAY EIGHT

ROLLING FOR FIVES AND TENS

Materials Needed

Class-size 10-bead Mathrack™

Individual 10-bead Mathrack™, one per pair of students

Small bags with approximately 20 dice in each. one bag per pair of students

Placemats, one per pair

Several sheets of copy paper and pencils for each group

Today begins with a minilesson using quick images on the Mathrack™. The string of related images is designed to support the development of prioritizing fives within numbers between 6 and 10. Afterwards, students are introduced to a new game: *Rolling for Fives and Tens.* They play two or three rounds in pairs, each time recording the matches they make that total 5 and 10. Each 5 counts as one point; each 10 counts as two points. The pair works to achieve a higher score than their scores in previous rounds.

Day Eight Outline

Minilesson: A String of Related Problems

❖ Use a string of related quick images on the 10-bead Mathrack™. Show one at a time and invite discussion of strategies.

Developing the Context

❖ Introduce the game *Rolling for Fives and Tens.*

Supporting the Investigation

❖ Students work in pairs playing *Rolling for Fives and Tens.* Provide each group with a set of cards and blank paper and pencils for recording the fives and tens they make.
❖ Confer with students as they play supporting the development of strategies and big ideas from the landscape in the Overview.

Minilesson: A String of Related Problems

Show one quick image at a time from the string below. The string is designed to move children away from counting and counting on strategies with an aim towards getting them to prioritize the 5 red beads as a group within the total. Ensure that you hold the rack correctly. The red beads should be on the children's left-hand side so that they are reading the amount from left to right, with the 5 red beads first.

The String:
5 red on the left
6 on the left
7 on the left
5 on the left
8 on the left
All 10 on the left
9 on the left

Inside One Classroom: A Portion of the Minilesson	
Anna (the teacher): Here is our first one. *(She shows 5 red.)* Ok, thumbs up when you are ready to share how many you saw. *(When most thumbs are up, Anna starts discussion.)*	
Jodi: I saw 5. I know because I counted: 1, 2, 3, 4, 5.	
Anna: *(Using the Mathrack™)* I know. I saw you counting. How many red beads are on the rack?	*Author's notes*
Jodi: 5.	
Anna: Good remembering. So I bet you didn't even need to count! Are there still 5 when I push all of them over?	*Anna starts with 5 red beads. She moves them all as a group. The way the string is crafted with related problems will support the prioritizing of the 5-structure.*
Jodi: Yes.	
Anna: So, we don't even need to count them then? Wow! That will make us fast! Ok. Be ready. Here's the next one. *(She shows 6 as 5 red and 1 white.)*	
Elsa: It's just 1 more. It was faster. I didn't count. I just said in my mind that 1 more was 6.	*The Mathrack™ is a helpful tool for thinking. Numbers to 10 can easily be seen as a group of 5 red beads, plus a small subitizable group of white beads.*
Anna: Wow! That was so great that you didn't need to count. You just knew that 5 and 1 more was 6. Ok, here is the next one. *(She shows 7.)* Don't forget to show me with a thumb when you are ready. *(Noticing that several students are still counting, Anna decides to have pair talk.)* Turn and talk to your elbow partner.	

(After a few minutes, Anna resumes whole group discussion.) **Anna:** Did anyone have an interesting partner who tried a really fast way? **Maya:** Hannah said it was just one more than the last one. We had 6 and 1 more was 7. **Anna:** One more than 6. So, before we had 5+1 and that was 6, and now we have 5+2 and that makes 7? We don't need to count? Wow, that is a fast way! *(Using the Mathrack™, Anna shows 6 as 5+1 and then adds 1 to make 7. She also separates the 5 red and 2 white a little so the children can see 5 and the subitizable unit of 2.)* Ok, here's the next one. *(She shows 5 and several students chorus, "5!")* **Anna:** Wow. Knowing 5 and using it is a great strategy! We'll get this strategy up on the strategy wall, too! Elsa, Maya, and Hannah's rule: "Don't count, use the 5 if you see it."	*Anna celebrates the emergence of the prioritizing of the 5 and declares a new jointly-authored strategy for the wall display.*

Developing the Context

After the minilesson, ask students to form a circle. Invite one child into the center with you and demonstrate how to play the game *Rolling for Fives and Tens.* The game is played with approximately 20 dice. Directions follow:

Rolling for Fives and Tens

Set-up: Players spread a placemat in the play area and empty the bag of approximately 20 dice onto it. All dice that roll off the placemat are put back in the bag. [The purpose of this rule is so children are encouraged to keep all the dice on the placemat and not to dump them wildly onto the table.]

Objective: To group numbers in ways that make 5 or 10.

Game Play:
- ❖ Using the numbers rolled when the bag was emptied, both players look for ways to group the dice on the placemat to make 5 or 10 and record their combinations.
- ❖ Each 5 made counts as one point. A group of 10 counts as two points.
- ❖ When no more 5s or 10s can be made, the score is totaled, and a new round begins.
- ❖ Each round, the pair works to achieve a higher score than their scores in previous rounds.

Once children understand how to play, provide materials to each pair: a bag of dice, a placemat, a Mathrack™ for checking the totals if they are not sure, a sheet of paper, and a pencil. Ask the students to play two or three rounds and keep track of the matches they find, trying to beat their earlier scores.

Supporting the Investigation

As children play, move around and confer. By this time, it is likely that many of your children will easily make groups of 5. For example, they may make 5 with 2+2+1, or with 5 ones, or they may just grab a 5. Remind them that making 10 earns two points and support them to think of ways to use the dice to make 10. Note their strategies. Do they only go after two 5s, or do they know that the 5 can be combined with a 2 and 3? Do they think of that group only as 5+5, or do they also see it as 7+3, or as 8+2? Support students to notice these equivalent expressions. If children focus on equivalence, there are almost no facts to memorize: 5+5 = 6+4 = 7+3 = 8+2.

Reflections on the Day

Math workshop began today again with a minilesson where students were encouraged to prioritize the 5 within numbers between 6 and 10. Doing so will help them image the facts that make 10, because the white beads can be broken into small, subitizable groups. For example, without the Mathrack™ most young children just learn to count on and they use this strategy for years without ever automatizing the basic facts. If 2 white beads are placed with the 5 red and children easily see this as 7, the 3 white beads remaining on the right are easily subitized, too, and thus 7+3 becomes easy. Working to achieve automatization of the facts within 10 is a goal and will be an important foundation to use when the 20-bead rack is introduced and used to help automatize the facts to 20. For example, if 7 is 5+2, then 7+7 is easily seen as 10+4. As students played *Rolling for Fives and Tens,* they were continuing to work with these relations. Tomorrow they will be challenged with a new game, a version of Go Fish, where they will need to ask for the missing addend.

DAY NINE

BARNYARD MATCH

Materials Needed

Class-size 10-bead Mathrack™

Cards for the game Barnyard Match (Appendix N, one set per pair of students)

Several sheets of copy paper and pencils for each group

Today begins with another minilesson, this time using a string of related addition and subtraction problems. The string is designed to support the prioritizing of the five-structure as a tool for thinking about combinations that make ten. Once again, the 10-bead Mathrack™ is used to represent students' strategies during discussion. Afterwards students are introduced to another new game: *Barnyard Match*.

Day Nine Outline

Minilesson: A String of Related Problems

❖ Using the class-size 10-bead Mathrack™, show one problem at a time from a string of related addition and subtraction problems and invite discussion of strategies.

❖ Use the Mathrack™ to represent student strategies.

Developing the Context

❖ Introduce the game *Barnyard Match.*

Supporting the Investigation

❖ Students work in pairs playing *Barnyard Match.* Provide each group with a set of cards and blank paper and pencils for recording matches.

❖ Confer with students as they play, supporting the development of strategies and big ideas from the landscape described in the Overview.

Minilesson: A String of Related Problems

Show one problem at a time from the string of problems below on the 10-bead Mathrack™, each time asking, "Who's missing?" Children need to answer by describing how many of Rhoda's chicks and how many of Loretta's chicks are missing and explain why they think this. The string is designed to support children to image the beads on the rack as a tool for missing addend problems. With each problem, you will be showing an image on the left side of the rack and hiding the remainder in your fist (or you can hide the remainder with a cloth or the small, white board that comes with the rack). As strategies are shared for determining the answer, use the rack and slide the beads to represent student thinking. If the answer is correct and all 10 beads are in place on the left, you and the children can say, "The gang's all here!"

The String:
5 red beads are shown; Who's missing?

4 red beads are shown; Who's missing?

6 beads (5 red and 1 white) are shown; Who's missing?

3 red beads are shown; Who's missing?

2 red beads are shown: Who's missing?

8 beads (5 red and 3 white) are shown: Who's missing?

1 red bead is shown: Who's missing?

Inside One Classroom: A Portion of the Minilesson	
Anna (the teacher): Here is our first one. *(She shows 5 red beads with the white beads hidden.)* Ok, who's missing? Thumbs up when you are ready to share. *(When most thumbs are up, Anna starts discussion.)* **Jodi:** It's 5. I know because… I just remember that one. **Anna:** Are the missing beads red or white? **Jodi:** White. I know because the rack has 5 reds and 5 whites. **Anna:** Like the chicks in the barnyard. Loretta's were hiding, but the gang is all here now! Here's the next one. *(She shows 4 red.)* Who's missing? **Eli:** I think Roy went over with Loretta's chicks to fool the fox. **Anna:** One of Rhoda's chicks is missing! So how many chicks are hiding? **Eli:** *(counts on)* 1, 2, 3, 4, 5, 6. Six. **Anna:** How many of Loretta's chicks are with Roy?	 *Author's notes* *Anna accepts that some of the facts are now becoming automatic. However, she probes to see if Jodi can image the full rack. This imaging of the 5-structure on the rack will be a helpful tool for her students as she goes on with the string, and as she works with her students to get the basic facts that make ten automatic.*

Eli: All of them. 5!

Anna: *(She shows the 6 hidden beads and then slides them over.)* 1 red bead and 5 white beads and that makes 6. You were right. And, I bet you didn't even need to count! 1 and 5 more is 6. And now the gang's all here! Here's the next one. *(She shows 5 red and 1 white, with 4 white hidden.)*

Harrison: Now 4 of Loretta's chicks are hiding. It's the same!

Anna: Tell us what you mean, Harrison.

Harrison: It was 4 red and 6 hiding before. Now it's 6, and 4 are hiding.

Anna: Wow! The old "switch-a-roo" again? That's a popular strategy. You used 4+6 to do 6+4?

The Mathrack™ is a helpful tool for thinking. Anna uses it here as a representational tool to illustrate the relations under discussion. Being able to image five as a group will eliminate the need to count. It will also support her students to see that 4+6 = 5+5.

Developing the Context

After the minilesson, ask students to form a circle. Invite one child into the center with you and demonstrate how to play the game *Barnyard Match*. Directions for making the cards can be found on Appendix J. Directions for playing are also shown below:

Barnyard Match

Set-up: All cards are placed face down in the center of the play area.

Objective: To make matches showing all 10 chicks.

Game Play:

❖ Players alternate choosing one card from the pile. The goal is to make a match and to exclaim, "The gang's all here!"

❖ The match must also make 5+5, meaning all 5 of Rhoda's chicks and all 5 of Loretta's chicks are shown. For example, if 4 red beads are shown, the match cannot be 1 white and 5 red, even though that combo makes 6. The card needed is 1 red and 5 white, because now we have 5+5 = 4+6. All 10 of the chicks are represented; the gang is all here.

❖ Once all matches are found, players check that they have all the cards by using the matches to make a staircase as shown and they record the expressions in order: 1+9; 2+8; 3+7; etc. as shown on the following page.

Once children understand how to play, provide pairs with a deck of cards and paper and pencils for recording.

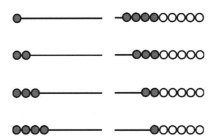

Figure 5. A Staircase of Expressions That Make 10.

Supporting the Investigation

As children play, move around and confer. Note the strategies children use to find the missing addend. Do they count on, count backwards, or do they just know the fact? If some children are still challenged and are counting, encourage them to use the Mathrack™ at the table for support.

Reflections on the Day

Math workshop began today again with a minilesson where students were encouraged to image the 10-bead Mathrack™ employing the use of the 5-structure as a helpful tool for missing addend problems. Then they were introduced to a new game: *Barnyard Match.* The game supported them to continue imaging the rack. Tomorrow a final game will be introduced for further encourage the prioritizing of five.

DAY TEN

FISH FOR TENS

Materials Needed

Class-size 10-bead Mathrack™

Individual 10-bead Mathracks™ (one per group of four students)

Cards for the game *Fish for Tens* (Appendix P, one set per group of four students)

Several sheets of copy paper and pencils for each group

Today begins with another minilesson. Like the one you did yesterday, it is focused on the development of strategies to find missing addends. Today, however, you will not show the rack, but will simply write the problem and ask students to tell you what they are imagining on the rack. As they share, represent their thinking on the 10-bead Mathrack™. Afterwards students are introduced to another new game: *Fish for Ten.* In this game they must envision the missing addend and ask for it.

Day Ten Outline

Minilesson: A String of Related Problems
❖ Write one problem at a time from a string of related problems, asking children to envision the rack. Invite discussion of strategies.
❖ Use the class-size 10-bead Mathrack™ to represent student strategies.

Developing the Context
❖ Introduce the game *Fish for Tens.*

Supporting the Investigation
❖ Students work in groups of four playing *Fish for Tens.* Provide each group with a set of cards and blank paper and pencils for recording matches.
❖ Confer with students as they play, supporting the development of strategies and big ideas from the landscape described in the Overview.

Minilesson: A String of Related Problems

Write one problem at a time from the string of problems below. After each problem, ask students to tell what they are imagining it would look like on the rack. As strategies are shared for determining the answer, use the 10-bead class-size Mathrack™ to represent student thinking. The purpose of imagining the rack is to remind students to use it as a tool for thinking. Initially the rack was a model of a situation—5 Rhode Island Red chicks and 5 Leghorn chicks. As the unit progressed the rack became a representational tool used by the teacher to represent problems and strategies. As the unit begins to close, we are starting the work of removing the rack, but encouraging children to still use it as a tool for thinking by envisioning the problem on it. If this is difficult for some, bring the rack back as support for those who still need it.

The String:

$$5 + \boxed{} = 10$$

$$9 + \boxed{} = 10$$

$$6 + \boxed{} = 10$$

$$4 + \boxed{} = 10$$

$$1 + \boxed{} = 10$$

$$7 + \boxed{} = 10$$

Inside One Classroom: A Portion of the Minilesson	
Anna (the teacher): Here is our first one. What would go in the box to make 10? How many are hiding in the box? I'm not going to show the rack today when I ask the problem unless we need it. Think about it, though. Put an image in your mind of what is on the rack to help you. Ok, thumbs up when you are ready to share. *(When most thumbs are up, Anna starts discussion.)* Pauline?	
Pauline: I'm thinking of 5 red beads on the rack and the 5 white beads moving over to be with them. And that makes 10.	*Author's notes*
Anna: *(Writes 5 in the box and, using the Mathrack™, she first pushes the 5 red beads in a group to the left, and then moves the remaining 5 white beads to the left as well, in one move as a group.)* Like this? That was a fast way, Pauline! Did anyone do it a different way? Yun? What was your way?	*Anna accepts that some of the facts are now becoming automatic for many, but she notices a few are still counting and she wants to get them to envision the rack.*
Yun: I thought of 5, too. Then I used my fingers and said 6, 7, 8, 9, 10.	

Anna: So, what goes in the box? If the 5 red chicks are there, how many other chicks are hiding? *(Yun shrugs, and looks puzzled.)* **Anna:** Let's look at that rack. You were imagining the 5 red beads, and then you used your fingers to count on? *(Yun nods in agreement.)* If I cover the rest of the beads up, we can pretend they are in the box. *(Anna covers the beads with a cloth.)* Do you know how many white beads are under there? **Yun:** 5. **Anna:** Did you just know that, or did you use your fingers again? **Yun:** I knew it. **Anna:** Wow!! You didn't even need to count? *(Yun beams.)* Look how the rack can help us. We don't even need to count! Nice job, Yun.	*Anna uses the Mathrack™ here as a representational tool to illustrate the relations under discussion. Since Yun counted, Anna falls back on the rack, asking Yun to imagine what is on it.* *Anna probes for clarification and then represents Yun's thinking on the Mathrack™, too.*

Developing the Context

After the minilesson, ask students to form a circle. Invite one child into the center with you and demonstrate how to play the game *Fish for Tens.* The game is played just like *Fish for Fives,* but this is a harder version, requiring children to ask for a card that will make 10 when placed with a card they have in their hand. The cards for this game are only numerals, which also makes it harder. Ensure children have individual 10-bead racks nearby in case they want to use them. Directions for making the cards and for playing can be found on Appendix K. Directions for playing are also shown below:

Fish for Tens

Set-up: All cards are placed in a face-down pile in the center of the playing area and each player chooses one card from the pile.

Objective: To match players' cards into equations that equal 10.

Game Play:

❖ One at a time, each player asks the group for the card he needs to make a total of 10 with the card in his hand. [For example, if the first player has a 3, he would ask the group if anyone has a 7.]

❖ If no one has the requested card, the asking player must choose a second card from the deck. If another player does have the number requested, she gives it to the requestor. If this player is left with no cards in her hand, she then chooses another card from the deck to use at her next turn.

- ❖ If the requestor received a card, the matching two cards are placed face up, so everyone can see the match that makes 10. If the match is not a correct one, the player keeps both cards, and the player to the left now becomes a requestor. If everyone agrees the match is a correct one and can justify that the total is 10 (a match), the requestor writes the equation on the recording sheet. [For example, "3+7 = 10."] Then he completes his turn by taking another card from the deck.
- ❖ Play continues like this unless a joker is drawn. When a joker is drawn, it can be used for any number needed, but the player must justify why that number works.
- ❖ The group's score is the number of equations they have made when all cards from the deck have been drawn.

Once children understand how to play, form groups of four students and provide materials to each group: a set of cards, a 10-bead Mathrack™, a sheet of paper, and a pencil.

Supporting the Investigation

As children play, move around and confer. Note the strategies children use to find the missing addend. Do they count on, count backwards, or do they just know the fact? There really are not many facts to memorize as compensation, commutativity, and prioritizing the 5 make them all easy. At this point in the unit, several students will likely know all the facts that make 10. But, there may still be some children who are challenged and still using counting strategies. As they play, encourage them to use the Mathrack™ at the table for support.

Reflections on the Unit

This unit was designed to be used early in kindergarten to develop the 5- and 10-structures. Humans have been prioritizing these structures in our cultures for millennia. Taoists believed that the number five was significant as it encompassed the five elements that make up the universe: fire, water, earth, wood, and metal. In music, five represents the perfect fifth, the first interval young children hear and sing and the basis for tuning most musical instruments. Fives and tens are the basis for many number systems developed around the world, including the decimal system in broad use today.

Now your young mathematicians are reveling in the power of five. They see fives everywhere, too—on their fingers and toes, in the barnyard with Rhoda and Loretta, and on the Mathrack™. And two 5s make a 10! It's quite probable that when you began this unit, you had several children not even able to count with meaning. Note how the early subitizable units of 1, 2, and 3 supported them in the first week of this unit. Getting the 5-structure solid with your students is an important accomplishment as it quickly became a new subitizable piece in the second week of the unit. Students worked to prioritize 5 as a group inside of the 10 and developed the ability to trust that it didn't need to be counted. In just ten short days you likely saw a lot of development with some students now even working towards automaticity of addition facts to 10.

Over the next several weeks (and months), continue to support the prioritizing of the 5. Encourage your students to see the 5 red beads on the rack as a group and to trust that they don't need to count the beads. Emphasize their use of equivalence and write equivalent expressions with the equal sign: 5+5 = 6+4. Have students continue to justify equivalence and soon you will find them easily able to substitute and exchange equivalent expressions. This work is very important as you are building a foundation for numeric fluency and even algebra!

This unit also contained several games. In kindergarten, games are an integral part of math workshop. Games can be used throughout the year and provide a powerful tool for differentiation. Many of the schools using CFLM also use DreamBox. During math workshop it is a common practice to have children working in small groups playing different games and/or working on computers using DreamBox. Think about how to organize an area in your room where the games can be easily accessible to the young hands and minds in your community.

Are you all here?

Mary Waesche Alessi
Cathy Fosnot

Illustration by Manuela Pentangelo

We dedicate this book to our
children and grandchildren,
who continually stimulate and
challenge us to keep
our minds creative.

Rhoda Red had 5 healthy, wonderful, fun-loving chicks.

They weren't always perfect, but she loved them with all her heart. "Ruby, Riley, Rose, Rubin and Roy...," Rhoda called out joyfully to her 5 chicks as she poked her head into the barn. "Are you all here?"

"Come on everyone, we're going into the barnyard to play. But remember, ... "

Rhoda cautioned them, "stay close, and don't go off on your own. I saw that crafty, old fox this morning, and he looked hungry!"

The 5 chicks lined up behind their mother and scurried into the yard.

Once in the barnyard, the chicks raced about scratching in the dirt to find some worms.

They were so involved in their search, they soon found themselves at different ends of the barnyard trying to determine who had found the juiciest worm.

Rhoda Red was carefully keeping an eye out for the crafty, old fox.

She turned around to make sure her babies were safe.

"Oh, no, no, no, no, no! What happened?" Rhoda Red screamed. Had the hungry fox taken one of her babies?

She knew they were all there when they walked to the barnyard in a straight line, but now things looked very different.

Rhoda called out in a worried voice, "Ruby, Riley, Rose, Rubin and Roy.... are you all here?"

Are they?

With a quizzical look, Ruby,
Riley, and Rose shouted,
"We're right here, Mom.
What's the matter?"

Rubin yelled, "I'm here, too!"
Roy yelled, too, but no one heard
him because he was a little busy.

"Oh, thank goodness, you are all here!"
Rhoda Red exclaimed.
"I thought for sure that fox
had come when I wasn't
looking and taken one of you."

Rhoda Red had been very worried, but now
she relaxed a little knowing all her 5
babies were there,
safe and sound.

here!

"Let's have a race to the stable," said Riley.

"OK," said Rose, "but I get a head start because I'm the smallest."

Ruby, Riley, Rubin and Roy got behind the starting line.

Rose moved a few chicken feet
ahead of the rest and when
everyone was in position,
she turned around and yelled,

"Mom, can you start the race?"

Rhoda turned around,
about to say "Go,"
but instead she said,
"Oh, no, no, no, no, no. Not again!"

They were all here before,
when she had seen 3 and 2
earlier, but now she saw
only 4 chicks on the
starting line,
with Rose out in front.

"Ruby, Riley, Rose, Rubin
and Roy...are you all here?"
Are they?

All the chicks yelled at once,
"Come on Mom! Stop worrying.
We're all here."
And so they were.

"Oh, thank goodness,
you are all here,"
exclaimed Rhoda with relief.
"I know that fox is around here
somewhere and I worry about you."

Rhoda Red took a deep breath and
began to relax. She got into character
as the referee and with her wing
poised high in the air,

she lowered it
quickly, yelling

"Go kids, go!"

Rose got an early lead,
but Ruby, Riley and Rubin
were close behind.
Roy... well, along the way he
had gotten a little distracted
and was at the back of the group.

Little Rose won the race by a
mere beak length in front of
her other siblings.

After the race, the chicks started laughing and talking about how their mother was acting so worried every time they formed different groups.

"Let's do it again," said Rose mischievously.

Ruby and Riley huddled together by the pig pen, while Rubin and Roy ducked behind the cow's legs.

In order to get their
mom's attention, Rose
threw a big rock into
a puddle and made
a big splash.

The sound of
the splash made
Rhoda Red jump!

She turned around so
fast she got dizzy
and fell down.

Looking up in horror,
she saw her chicks grouped
differently again.

"Oh, no, no, no, no, no!" She yelled.
    "Not again!"
She was certain the fox had come this time
and taken one of her babies. With fear in her
voice, she slowly called out, "Ruby, Riley, Rose,
Rubin and Roy ... are you all here?"

    Are they?

Ruby, Riley, Rose, Rubin and Roy were all hysterical.

They were laughing so hard they could hardly breathe.

Finally, Rose calmed down enough to say, "We're all here Mom. Don't worry."

All 5 chicks were
safe and sound and
Rhoda was relieved.
But, she did not appreciate
their antics!
"It's not funny! I've had enough!"
she said with a frown.
"I thought for sure the fox had come and
taken one of you away."

"Everyone come here,"
Rhoda demanded.

With her 5 babies safely tucked under her wings, Rhoda Red thought about all the ways her chicks had grouped themselves together.

"I get it now," she thought. "There are many way they can group themselves. Just because they changed groups doesn't mean that I had lost any of them to that nasty fox. They were here the whole time."

"OK,"
said Rhoda Red,
"everybody, back to the barn."
Ruby, Riley, Rose, Rubin and Roy
all raced back to the barn shouting,
"Last one in eats a stinky bug."

Rhoda Red watched as 4 of her
babies sprinted into the barn.
She looked back to see Roy,
as usual, slowly making his
way back to the barn.

"Well," said Rhoda,
"there are 4 in the barn
and 1 slow poke.

But this time ...
I know all my babies are safe
and sound, because 4 + 1 makes 5.
All my chicks are here.
I'm not going to worry about the fox this time."

Should she be worried?

"That's strange," said Rhoda. She had an odd feeling that something just wasn't right. Just to be sure, she decided to count her babies one more time. She had each chick call out a number.

"1," said Ruby.
"2," said Riley.
"3," said Rose.
"4," said Rubin.
"5," said Roy.

"OK, so now I know all my babies
are here, safe and sound,"
said Rhoda.

"But wait! What's this?
There's one more!
What??"
shouted Rhoda.

"I don't have 6 baby chicks!"

"Oh, no, no, no, no, no!
No, you don't!!"

Printed in the United States of America
First Printing, 2017

ISBN-10: 0-9976886-5-3
ISBN-13: 978-0-9976886-5-8

Catherine Fosnot and Associates
New Perspectives on Learning, LLC
www.newperspectivesonlearning.com

About the Authors

Mary Waesche Alessi is a Registered Nurse by profession, but she also holds a degree in Early Childhood Education. With 5 preschool and kindergarten aged grandchildren, who all listen to and love her storytelling, Mary quickly discovered that she had a talent for weaving math learning opportunities into her stories with creative, fun, imaginative story lines. *Are You All Here?* is her first published book for children. She is currently working on a sequel, *The Gang's All Here.*

Mary Waesche Alessi

Cathy Fosnot is Professor Emerita of Childhood Education from CCNY, where she was the founder of the acclaimed center, Mathematics in the City. She has authored numerous books and articles on mathematics education, most recently *Conferring with Young Mathematicians at Work: Making Moments Matter* and the *Contexts for Learning Mathematics* series, K-6, a curriculum used widely by schools around the world. In 2004 she received the Teacher of the Year award from CCNY. Currently she serves as the senior content consultant for the award-winning internet math environment, DreamBox Learning, and is the President of New Perspectives on Learning, New Perspectives Online, and New Perspectives on Assessment. She resides in New London, CT, where she frequently offers workshops with her team at Ocean Beach.

Cathy Fosnot

About the Illustrator

Manuela Pentangelo is an illustrator who loves to paint and create. Her passion for illustration has led her to have more than 40 published children's books available in many countries around the world and in many formats (print, animations, online, tablet). Her style is a combination of traditional and digital painting. She lives and works on The Island of the Island, a small island off the coast of Sardinia.

Manuela Pentangelo

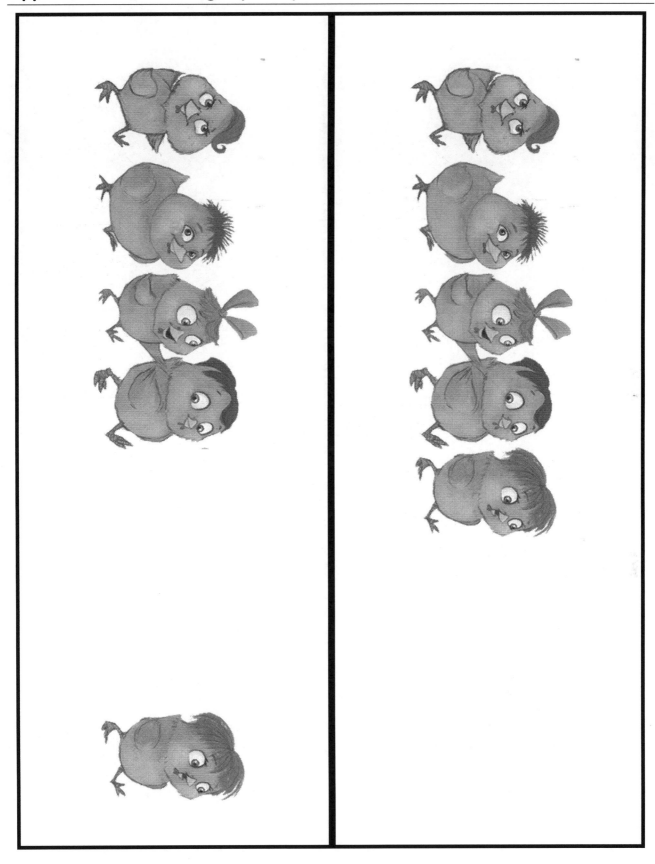

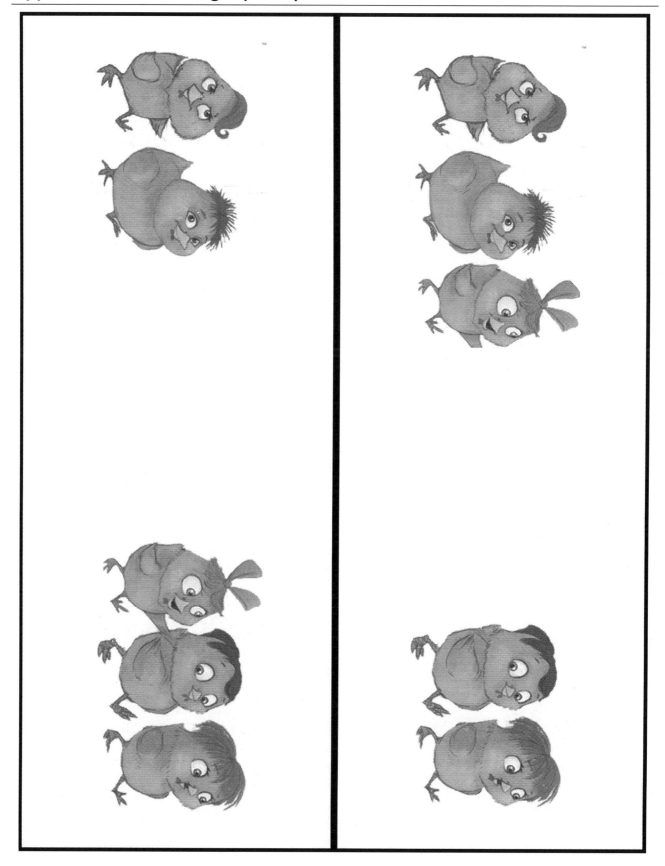

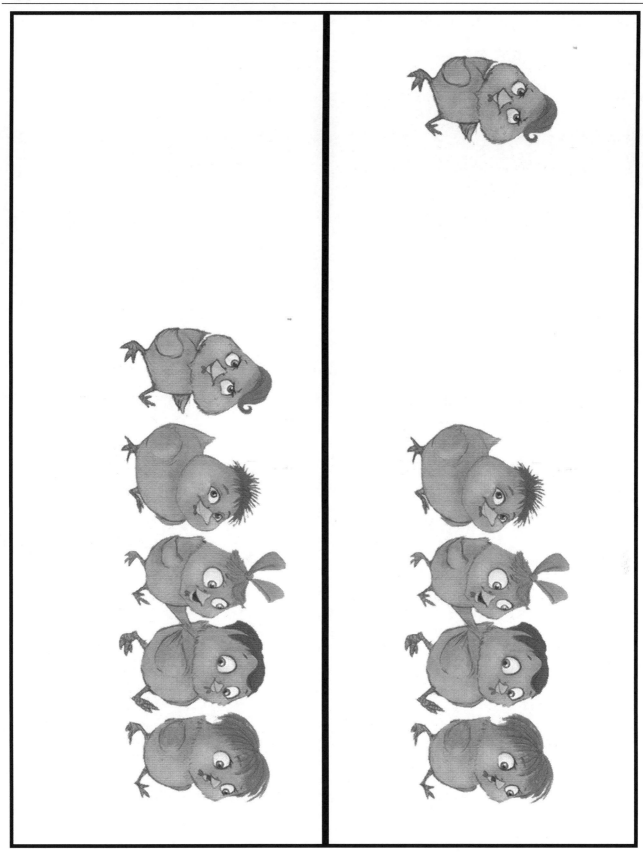

Appendix D – Directions for playing *Finding Five Chicks*

Set-up: All cards of the chicks are laid out face down in the center of the playing area in an array, 4 rows of 4.

Objective: To make matches showing all 5 of Rhoda's chicks.

Game Play:

- ❖ Play is cooperative as players work to make as many groups of 5 as they can.
- ❖ Players take turns turning over one card and laying it face up. If it is a match with another face-up card to make all 5 of Rhoda's chicks (**looking carefully to make sure there aren't duplicates of the same chick— 5 different chicks are needed**), the matching cards are removed from the center and placed face-up in a row next to each other.
- ❖ Players continue taking turns picking a card and together they make as many matches as possible.

Children can write the expressions they make on a recording sheet if they wish. It is likely that the commutative property will appear and can become the starting point for a discussion.

For example, it is probable that children will find the following matches:

3 + 2

2 + 3

1 + 4

4 + 1

As you confer, you might consider asking children to justify why 3 + 2 = 2 + 3 and 1 + 4 = 4 + 1. Encourage them to justify why order doesn't matter.

Appendix E – Cards for *Finding Five Chicks*

Printing instructions: Make two copies of the following cards for each deck and cut along the lines, resulting in 16 cards per deck.

Appendix F – Directions for playing *Fish for Fives*

Set-up: All cards are placed in a face-down pile in the center of the playing area and each player chooses one card from the pile.

Objective: To match players' cards into equations that equal 5.

Game Play:

- ❖ One at a time, each player asks the group for the card he needs to make a total of 5 with the card in his hand. [For example, if the first player has a 3, he would ask the group if anyone has a 2.]

- ❖ If no one has the requested card, the asking player must choose a second card from the deck. If another player does have the number requested, she gives it to the requestor. If this player is left with no cards in her hand, she then chooses another card from the deck, but she has to wait until her next turn to use it.

- ❖ If the requestor received a card, the matching two cards are placed face up, so everyone can see the match that makes 5. If the match is not a correct one, the player keeps both cards, and the player to the left now becomes a requestor. If everyone agrees the match is a correct one and can justify that the total is 5 (a match), the requestor writes the equation on the recording sheet. [For example, he would write "3+2 = 5."] Then he completes his turn by taking another card from the deck.

- ❖ Play continues like this unless a 5 or a joker is drawn. Whenever a 5 is drawn, the player takes some little squares (1-4, player's choice) out of the envelope and covers up a corresponding amount on the 5. The remaining amount becomes the card requested, and a smart move is to make a card in the player's hand usable. [For example, if a player uses 3 squares to cover 3 hearts, she requests a 2, but if the player has a 2 in her hand she can use it instead of requesting from the other players.] If a 2 is produced, the equation written is 5 – 3 = 2. If no one has a 2, a card is drawn from the deck and the turn passes to the next player.

- ❖ When a joker is drawn, it can be used for any number needed, but the player must justify why that number works.

- ❖ The group's score is the number of equations they have made when all cards from the deck have been drawn.

Appendix G: Cards for *Fishing for Fives*

Printing instructions: Make four copies of the following cards for each deck (you will have two extra Jokers) and cut along the lines, resulting in 22 cards per deck and plenty of little square chicks.

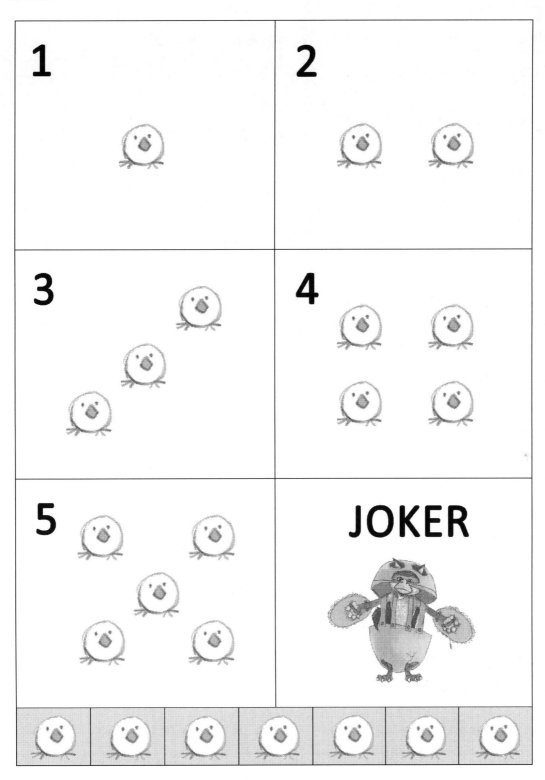

Appendix H – Directions for playing *Building Equations*

Set-up: All cards are placed face-up in the middle of the table. Players will also use a 6-sided die in which the 6 has been covered by a white dot or other obscuring sticker.

Objective: To build and capture expressions equivalent to 5.

Game Play:

- ❖ During the first round, each player takes a turn to roll the die and a card that matches it. [For example, if a player rolls a 4, she chooses a card with 4 beads on it and places it face-up in front of her. If the white dot is rolled, the player may choose any number.] Now all players each have one card.

- ❖ On the second and later rounds, the roll of the die may produce a card that makes a total of 5 when placed with one of the player's existing cards. If this is the case, the player gets to take a plus sign and builds an expression that is equal to 5. [For example, at this point a player might have 3+2, if he already had a 3 and he just rolled a 2.]

- ❖ Play continues in turns with players building expressions equivalent to 5 when they can. If at any point a player rolls a 5, she takes a 5-card from the table and uses it to capture an equivalent expression from the table. The player puts the expression in the envelope, recording the equation on the group's scorecard, then places the 5-card back on the table. [If she captured 3+2, she would write 3+2 = 5, and would place the 3 and 2 cards in the envelope and the 5-card back on the table.]

- ❖ When the die rolled has a blank face (white dot), a player can use it to be any number he needs. [He might want it to be a 5 so he can capture an equivalent expression, or he might want it to serve for a missing addend, so he can make an expression and take a plus sign.]

- ❖ The objective is to get all the 1-4 cards back in the envelope. The group's final score is the number of equations they build.

Printing instructions: Make five copies of the following cards for each deck and cut along the lines, resulting in 25 number cards per deck.

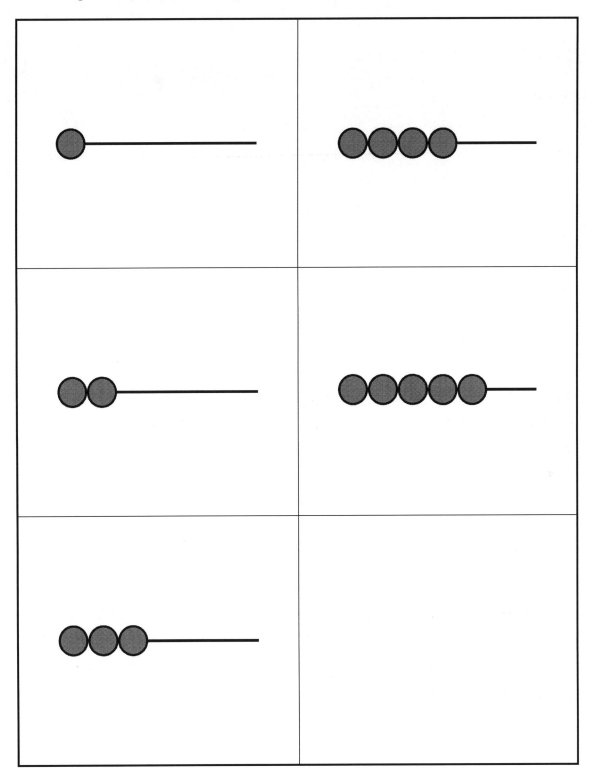

Printing instructions: Make one copy of the following cards for each set of number cards and cut along the lines, resulting in 10 plus signs for each deck.

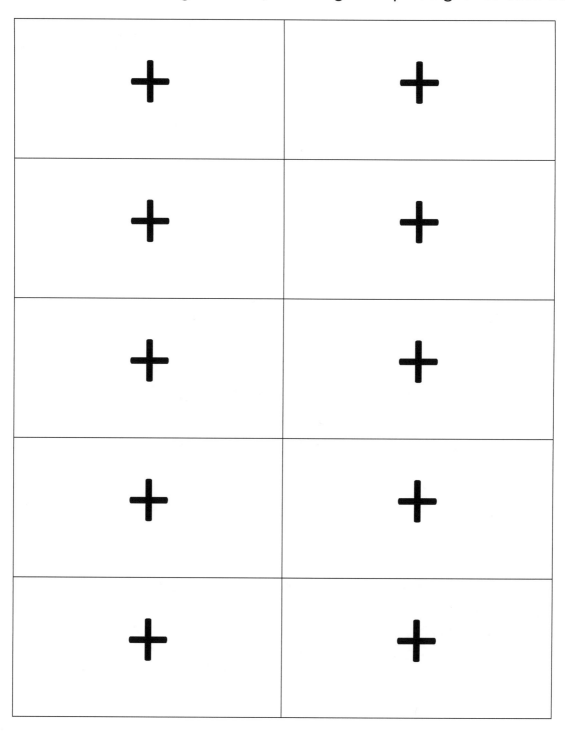

The Gang's All Here

Mary Waesche Alessi
Cathy Fosnot

Illustration by Manuela Pentangelo

We dedicate this book to our children and grandchildren, who continually stimulate and challenge us to keep our minds creative.

"Ugh, I hope these chicks come soon," Loretta Leghorn thought to herself. "It's like sitting on a bunch of hard lumpy rocks. My bottom is sore."

Rhoda Red came into the barn all excited for her friend Loretta. "Anything yet?" she asked.

"No!" groaned Loretta. She wiggled her bottom trying to get more comfortable. "I hope they come soon."

Rhoda couldn't wait for her friend to have chicks of her own. She looked over with pride at her own 5 chicks: Ruby, Riley, Rose, Rubin, and Roy. She knew how lucky she was to have them. She imagined how much fun the two families would have together and of course there would be more eyes to watch out for that nasty old fox!

Suddenly Loretta's eyes got big and wide. In an excited voice she yelled, "Oh my. Ohhhhh my! Something is tickling my feathers. Oh my goodness. My babies are here!"

Flying off the eggs, Loretta looked down at the nest. There, sitting amongst the hay, loose feathers, and broken egg shells, sat 5 precious baby Leghorn chicks.

Ruby, Riley, Rose, Rubin, and Roy all rushed to the edge of the nest. They were very excited to see their new friends.

"What are their names?" Rose asked.

"Everyone!" announced Loretta. "I am proud to introduce to you: Lilly, Lucy, Lola, Larry, and Lou."

Rhoda gave her friend a big hug and immediately started to advise her on how to care for her chicks. At the same time, Rhoda's chicks each took hold of one of their new friends and began to show the new buddy around the barn.

They showed them where the farmer tossed out the food for them to eat and where the best watering hole was to drink.

They showed them the difference between the black and white barn cat and the mean, stinky skunk. Most importantly, they told the new chicks to make sure to keep an eye out for the crafty old fox.

As the chicks were all getting to know each other, Rhoda was enjoying the company of her friend. She and Loretta were chatting about proper chick bedtimes, good food choices, and the importance of being on the lookout for the fox.

At the thought of the fox, Loretta looked down at the nest to make sure her children were safe, but instead of seeing her babies, all she saw was an empty nest with broken egg shells. "Oh no, no, no, no, no! They're gone!" she yelled.

Loretta cried out, "Lilly, Lucy, Lola, Larry, Lou... where are you?" She turned around, and looking around the barn, she noticed that each chick had paired, each with one of Rhoda's chicks. But were they all there?

Is the gang of 10 all there?

The older chicks looked up in surprise. "It's OK, Mrs. Leghorn," said Rubin. "We each have one of your chicks. There are 5 of us, so there are 5 of your chicks here. We're just showing your babies around the barn."

Is Rubin right? Are there 5 Leghorn chicks?

Loretta wasn't sure so she counted them. Yes! 5 Rhode Island Red chicks and 5 white Leghorn chicks. The gang was all there. "Thank goodness you're all here," said Loretta. "I'm new at being a mother and I worry about that fox your mother was telling me about."

Just then Loretta's chicks noticed that Roy had wandered off into the barnyard and was digging a big hole. They ran over to see what he was doing. He was setting another trap to catch the fox.

Ruby, Rose, Rubin, and Riley were hungry and so they went back towards the barn to see if they could find some leftover corn.

Rhoda and Loretta had been busy talking about their chicks. They looked up from the doorway of the barn.

"Oh no, no, no, no, no!" exclaimed Loretta. "Rhoda, you only have 4 chicks!"

Is the gang of 10 all there?

All the chicks turned to face their mothers. Well, all except Roy that is, because he was laying out another trap for the fox.

"Mom," the chicks all said together, "the gang's all here!"

"Phew," said Loretta. "Keeping track of these chicks is nerve-wracking."

"You have no idea," said Rhoda. "Just wait until you experience your first fox sighting. Then things can get really crazy!"

Roy walked over to the water trough to get a drink of water and got another idea about how he could capture the fox. He started drilling a hole in the side of the trough. Rose and Rubin went over to see what he was doing.

Loretta looked up and now she saw only 2 of Rhoda's chicks. "Wait... What... Where are they?" she yelled. "Oh no! Children, are you all here?"

Is the gang all here?

The chicks thought their moms' reactions were funny. Laughing, Ruby said, "We're all here. Don't worry."

Larry thought this was hilarious. "Let's do it again and see what they do this time," he said.

Lilly, Lucy, Lola, Larry, and Lou all ran toward the barn, while Riley, Rose, and Rubin hid by the cow. In order to get their moms to look, Riley pulled at the cow's tail, causing it to let out a loud, "Moooo."

Loretta and Rhoda turned at the sound of the cow.
"Oh no, no, no, no, no!" exclaimed the mothers with concern.
"Are all of our 10 chicks here?"

Are they?

Both moms looked on as their chicks laughed
hysterically. "Alright you little rascals," said Rhoda.
"No more funny business. Everyone come here."

All 10 chicks lined up near their mothers: Rhoda's 5
chicks on the left, and Loretta's 5 chicks on the right.

Rhoda tried to sound angry, but her words came out in a giggle. "We're on to you now. You can't trick us anymore."

Loretta added, "You've created all sorts of different groups, but we know now, you were all always here."

Can you think of any other ways to group the chicks?

"OK," said Rhoda. "Everyone back to the barn. It's almost dinner time and I'm hungry."

"Me too! Whew! What a day!" exclaimed Loretta. She flung open the heavy barn door to let everyone in and heard a grunt.
"What was that? Barn doors don't say Ouch!" Loretta got a little nervous and called out to Rhoda, "Are all the chicks here?"

Rhoda answered, "Let's count to be safe. Ok everyone, sound off."

"1," said Lilly.
"2," said Lucy.
"3," said Lola.
"4," said Larry.
"5," said Lou.

"Well, all 5 of my chicks are here," thought Loretta.

"6," said Ruby.
"7," said Riley.
"8," said Rose.
"9," said Rubin.

"Oh no! Where's Roy!" Rhoda yelled. "Roy, where are you?" She knew he had been trying to set traps for the fox all day. Had the fox captured him instead???

Then Rhoda saw Roy,
dillydallying in the barnyard with a
frustrated look on his face. She thought
to herself, "....Hmmm, there are 9 already
in the barn and Roy makes 1 more.
That makes 10: 5 of Loretta's chicks,
and 5 of my own."

As Rhoda walked over to her son, he said, "Mom, can't I stay out a little while longer? I've been setting traps for the fox all day and I haven't caught him yet."

Rhoda put her wing around Roy and said. "I know you have, my brave little chick-a-dee and I'm so proud of you. But it's getting late and it's time to come inside now. Tomorrow's another day."

As Rhoda and Roy entered the barn, Loretta started to close the heavy door for the night.

"Wait!" Loretta said, looking out. "Did you hear that?"

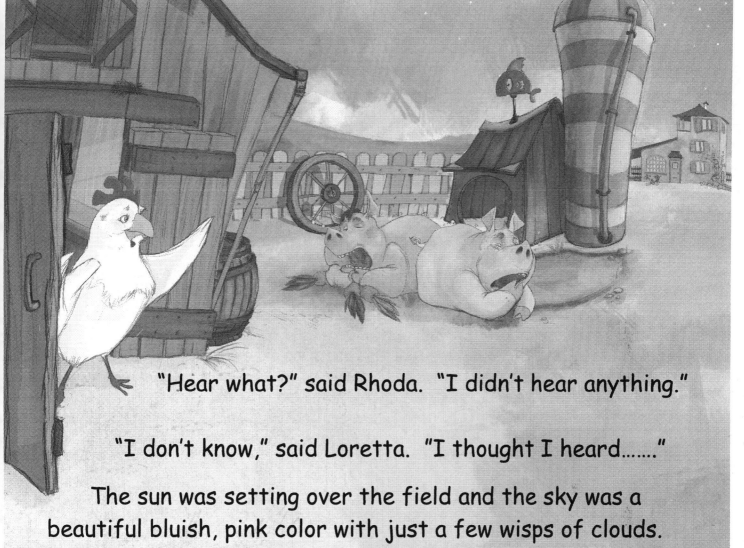

"Hear what?" said Rhoda. "I didn't hear anything."

"I don't know," said Loretta. "I thought I heard......."

The sun was setting over the field and the sky was a beautiful bluish, pink color with just a few wisps of clouds. Loretta looked out across the barnyard. She thought how lucky she was to be raising her baby chicks in such a beautiful, quiet, peaceful setting. With a gentle sigh Loretta said, "Nope, nothing there. Come on! Now that the gang's all here, let's eat!"

First Printing, 2018

ISBN-13: 978-0-9976886-9-6

Catherine Fosnot and Associates
New Perspectives on Learning, LLC
www.newperspectivesonlearning.com

Appendix K – The 10 Chicks

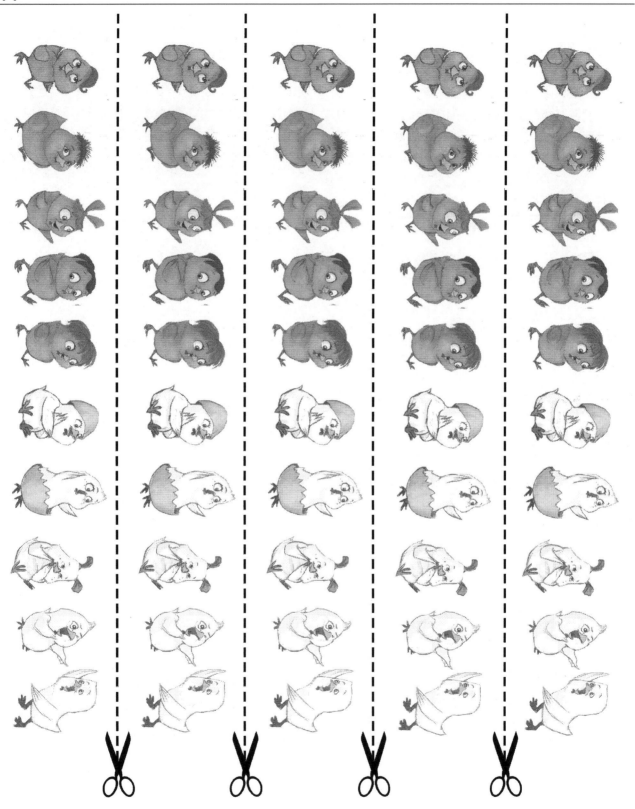

Appendix L – Directions for *Rolling for Fives and Tens*

Set-up: Players spread a placemat in the play area and empty the bag of approximately 20 dice onto it. All dice that roll off the placemat are put back in the bag. [The purpose of this rule is so children are encouraged to keep all the dice on the placemat and not to dump them wildly onto the table.]

Objective: To group numbers in ways that make 5 or 10.

Game Play:

❖ Using the numbers rolled when the bag was emptied, both players look for ways to group the dice on the placemat to make 5 or 10 and record their combinations.

❖ Each 5 made counts as one point. A group of 10 counts as two points.

❖ When no more 5s or 10s can be made, the score is totaled, and a new round begins.

Each round, the pair works to achieve a higher score than their scores in previous rounds.

Appendix M – Directions for *Barnyard Match*

Set-up: All cards are placed face down in the center of the play area.

Objective: To make matches showing all 10 chicks.

Game Play:

❖ Players alternate choosing one card from the pile. The goal is to make a match and to exclaim, "The gang's all here!"

❖ The match must also make 5+5, meaning all 5 of Rhoda's chicks and all 5 of Loretta's chicks are shown. For example, if 4 red beads are shown, the match cannot be 1 white and 5 red, even though that combo makes 6. The card needed is 1 red and 5 white, because now we have 5+5 = 4+6. All 10 of the chicks are represented; the gang is all here.

❖ Once all matches are found, players check that they have all the cards by using the matches to make a staircase as shown and they record the expressions in order: 1+9; 2+8; 3+7; etc.

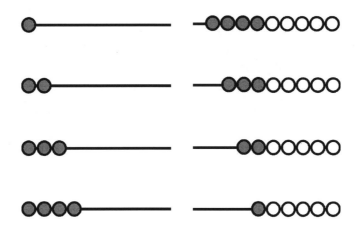

Etc.

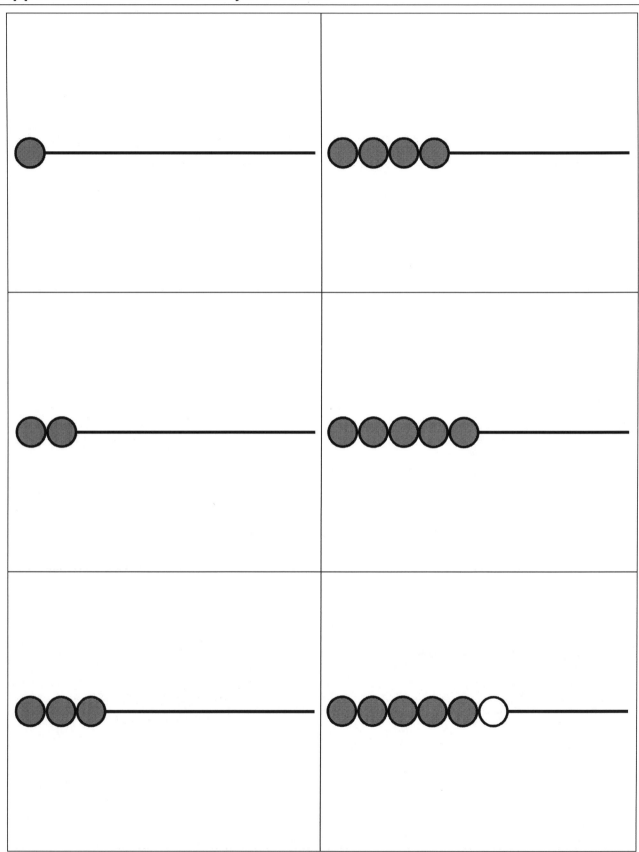

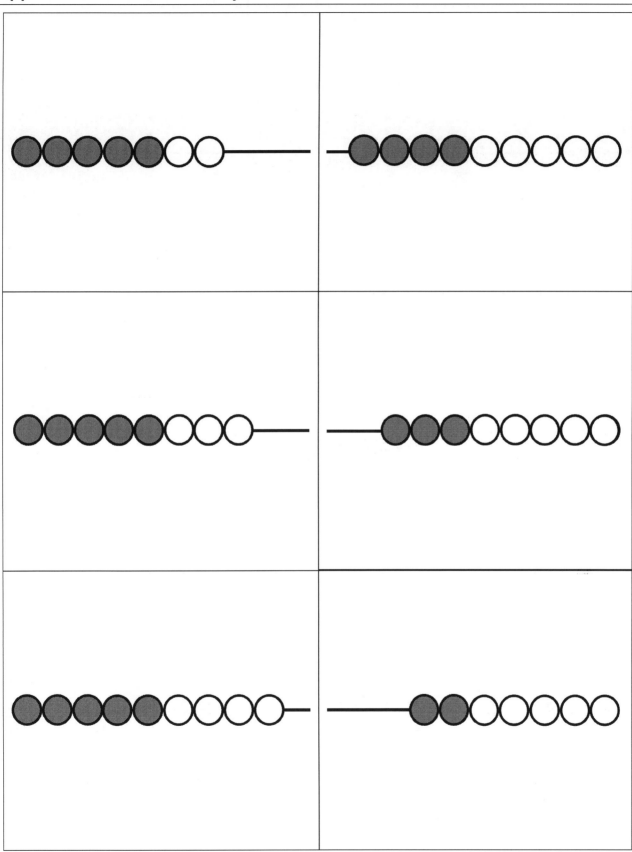

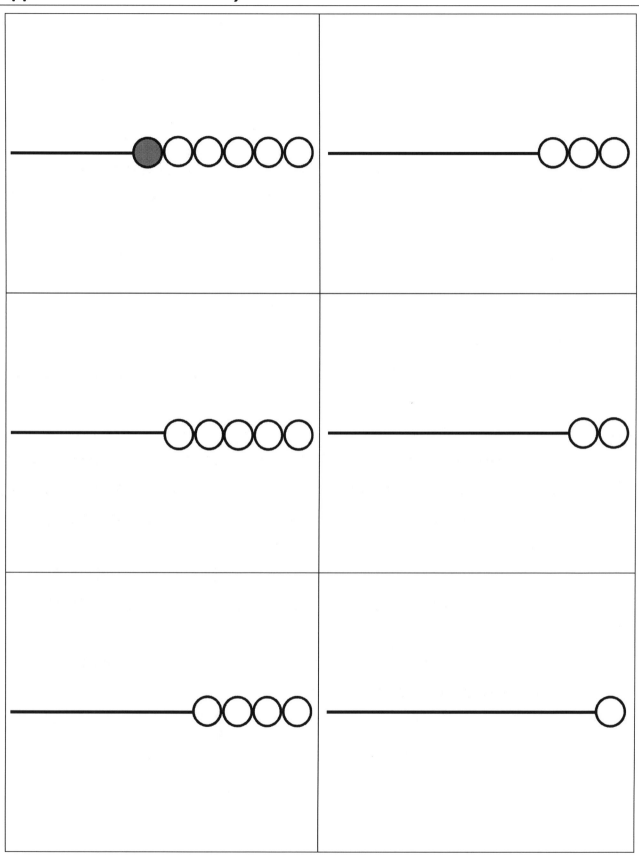

Appendix O: Directions for *Fish for Tens*

Set-up: All cards are placed in a face-down pile in the center of the playing area and each player chooses one card from the pile.

Objective: To match players' cards into equations that equal 10.

Game Play:

❖ One at a time, each player asks the group for the card he needs to make a total of 10 with the card in his hand. [For example, if the first player has a 3, he would ask the group if anyone has a 7.]

❖ If no one has the requested card, the asking player must choose a second card from the deck. If another player does have the number requested, she gives it to the requestor. If this player is left with no cards in her hand, she then chooses another card from the deck to use at her next turn.

❖ If the requestor received a card, the matching two cards are placed face up, so everyone can see the match that makes 10. If the match is not a correct one, the player keeps both cards, and the player to the left now becomes a requestor. If everyone agrees the match is a correct one and can justify that the total is 10 (a match), the requestor writes the equation on the recording sheet. [For example, "3+7 = 10."] Then he completes his turn by taking another card from the deck.

❖ Play continues like this unless a joker is drawn. When a joker is drawn, it can be used for any number needed, but the player must justify why that number works.

❖ The group's score is the number of equations they have made when all cards from the deck have been drawn.

Appendix P: Cards for *Fish for Tens*

Printing instructions: Make three copies of the following cards for each deck and cut along the lines, resulting in 33 cards per deck.

1	2
3	4
5	6

7	8
9	10
Joker	

95813602R00084

Made in the USA
Middletown, DE
27 October 2018